The busy girl's guide to
SEWING

Unlock your inner sewing goddess:
projects, advice and inspiration for a creative lifestyle

Carrie Maclennan

David and Charles
www.rucraft.co.uk

For my parents, Jim and Kathleen McMonagle.
Thanks for instilling in me the spirit of DIY.

A DAVID & CHARLES BOOK
© F&W Media International LTD 2011

David & Charles is an imprint of F&W Media International LTD
Brunel House, Forde Close, Newton Abbot, TQ12 4PU, UK

F&W Media International LTD is a subsidiary of F+W Media, Inc.
4700 East Galbraith Road, Cincinnati, OH 45236

First published in the UK and US in 2011

Text and designs © Carrie Maclennan 2011
Layout and photography © F&W Media International LTD 2011

Carrie Maclennan has asserted her right to be identified as author
of this work in accordance with the Copyright, Designs and Patents Act, 1988.

A catalogue record for this book is available from the British Library.

ISBN-13: 978-0-7153-3868-1 paperback
ISBN-10: 0-7153-3868-4 paperback

Printed in China by RR Donnelley
for F&W Media International LTD
Brunel House, Forde Close, Newton Abbot, TQ12 4PU, UK

Publisher Alison Myer
Acquisitions Editor Jennifer Fox-Proverbs
Editor James Brooks
Project Editor Ame Verso
Senior Designer Mia Trenoweth
Photographer Garry Maclennan
Illustrations Ethan Danielson
Senior Production Controller Kelly Smith

David & Charles publish high quality books on a wide range of subjects.
For more great book ideas visit: www.rucraft.co.uk

CONTENTS

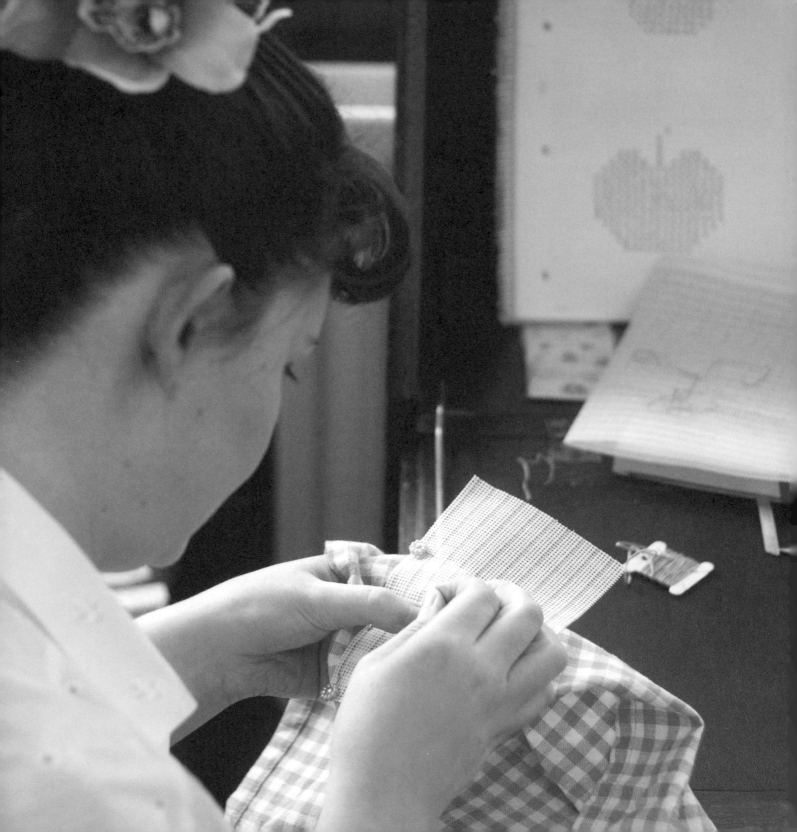

INTRODUCTION

Yes. It's true. I'm 31 years old. I've been working in the creative industries promoting indie craft and design for many years – but am only now just learning to sew on a button. There. I said it.

Now, this late arrival to the ancient sewing circle does not mean I haven't been thinking about sewing. No, no. Why, in my head I've redesigned unwanted clothes, I've repaired and replaced zips and buttons, and I've stitched up all manner of home accessories. In real life though, I've mainly been folding tatty wardrobe rejects into suitcases labelled, 'to fix' and hoarding lengths and lengths of fabric in laundry bags only to store them out of reach then forget all about them until it's time for spring cleaning again.

Most of the sewing books you already have in your collection are most likely penned by seasoned professionals – talented designer-makers and crafty

types who know their way around a sewing machine and can whip up a party frock with their eyes shut and one hand tied behind their backs. Until I began writing this book, my relationship with sewing machines was fraught. Hampered by deep-seated fear and anxiety thanks to dreadful memories of a pencil case disaster in Home Economics class back in 1992, my sewing skills leave a lot to be desired. Or, at least, they did.

This book maps my journey from sewing-phobic scaredy cat to self-assured stitcher in just three tightly packed chapters. En route, I have gathered together a collection of 13 sewing projects to share with you. Each one has been kindly contributed by designer-makers whose vim and verve, talent and passion for sewing has inspired me to shed my sewing hang-ups and reconnect with my inner sewing goddess. Apparently I do have one! From homewares and accessories to craft kit essentials and wearables, I am certain you will love them.

Despite my rather unusual author status as 'novice', the projects in the book are well suited to busy sewers of varying experience. I would recommend working through the projects in chapter order if you are in the early stages of getting to grips with a needle and thread. If you are already in tune with this sewing lark, then you might prefer to dip in and out of the book as and when you feel like it –

completing a project whenever you can squeeze in the time. There is no 'right way' to do things.

The makers I've worked with on this book are so immersed in their creative endeavours that the practicalities of making a skirt or a bag are instinctive – not prescriptive. This book embraces spontaneity and imperfection. It encourages you to experiment with techniques and urges you to customize and adapt each project further and really make it your own. Think of the project as a starting point, a preliminary exercise to get your creative self in gear – then see where you end up!

Designed specifically with busy girls in mind, the 13 projects presented here have been grouped together according to the blocks of time required to complete them. If you have just half an hour spare and are yearning for that satisfaction of starting and completing a project in one sitting, without having to

think too hard, then chapter 1 is for you. However, if your schedule allows you a quiet hour away from the usual hustle and bustle of a busy day and you can spend some quality time with your sewing machine, then chapter 2 is chock-full of project ideas for you to start and finish in one go. Managed to set aside an entire afternoon for a glorious, indulgent sewing session? Great! The projects in chapter 3 take four hours (or less) to complete and are ideal for when you have time to really sink yourself into a sewing task. However, if you're already wondering how on earth you will ever slot in a four-hour break to whip up a project, worry not! The more complex and time-consuming projects in chapter 3 have been conveniently 'chunked' into manageable blocks, allowing you to work through them little by little when you have a free moment. Swell, huh?

Peppered throughout the book, you will also find a number of magazine-style feature articles. Focused more on indie craft and vintage lifestyle than on project work, these sections serve as little interludes in your sewing schedule. Whether you are starting out and looking to get connected to the online craft community or you have aspirations of one day setting up shop at a craft fair, you will enjoy flipping through the features during your break time.

Before We Begin...

This is a project book, a lifestyle book and all-round handy resource. However, it isn't designed as an all-encompassing 'how-to' guide to sewing or to using your sewing machine. For you to get the most from the book, I am assuming that you already know how to thread your machine, wind the bobbin and use the machine's basic functions. If you don't – don't panic. Just dig out the manufacturer's instructions and work your way through, step by step. If you've been lucky enough to pick up a bargain reconditioned machine and it doesn't have a manual, then look up the make and model number online – I bet you will find one! If all else fails, call in the help of a sewing-savvy pal to show you the basics.

GETTING STARTED

Whether you are dusting off a neglected sewing kit, reviving a hand-me-down craft box or starting from scratch to build a shiny new one, enjoy the process of gathering your tools and materials. I am such a sucker for a pretty sewing supply. Won over by vintage packaging, a beautiful label or a gorgeous colourway, I find myself now living in a house full of sewing ephemera that, I have recently learned, is pretty much defunct and so now essentially decorative. Check and double check that you have all the basics of a good quality sewing kit from the off and you will never be caught short halfway through a project. A bit like cooking up a batch of Bolognese only to find you forgot to buy tomatoes, you will wind up frustrated and grumpy if your sewing kit lets you down midway through making something.

If buying new, choose good-quality, value tools that you feel comfortable using. Don't be wooed by

overly expensive novelty items or complicated gizmos. You will find a massive selection of useful items on offer. Don't be intimidated by the sheer choice available and don't be duped into buying loads of notions you will have little use for in the long term. If, like me, you don't know your seam ripper from your rotary cutter, enlist the help of

a clued-up crafty chum and ask if they'd tag along with you when you buy your kit. And, if you just can't resist the temptation of the floral shears or vintage-style measuring tape in the beautiful box, then go ahead and treat yourself. I have dedicated an area of wall in my house to displaying all the pretty (though not necessarily usable) sewing items I've accumulated!

Take a list with you when you visit the supplies shop. Or – to save time and energy – buy online from your desk and have everything delivered straight to your door in one neat package.

Basic Tools for Hand Sewing

Pins You will need a good stock of straight pins for all sorts of projects. Keep plenty to hand.

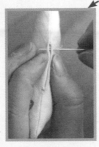

Needles Invest in a jumbo pack containing different sized needles with different sized eyes, as well as embroidery needles, which have a blunter point than general sewing needles.

Fabric scissors No, you can't just use your everyday household scissors for your textile projects! Buy a pair of good-quality shears – and make sure you keep them with your sewing kit. Make it clear to everyone in your house that these babies are for fabric use only!

Paper scissors To save blunting your fancy new fabric scissors, buy a second pair of scissors for working with paper, cutting pattern templates and so on.

Pinking shears My favourite of all my sewing tools so far. Invest in a good pair of pinking shears to eliminate the need for overlocking cotton fabrics and for creating easy decorative edges.

Embroidery scissors Not only do embroidery scissors tend to be pretty, but with their sharp, fine points, they will offer no end of help when you need to get down to some fiddly trimming.

Tape measure An absolute must-have. Make sure your tape measure is flexible – but not stretchy. Sometimes fabric tapes stretch over time so stock up on spares or invest in a heavy-duty plastic one.

Threads To start off your collection, get hold of a multi-pack of good quality threads in a range of common colours making sure you have a good stock of black, white, brown, grey and navy just for starters. Expand your thread tin rainbow reel by reel. You will also need stranded cotton (floss) for embroidery.

- **Cutting mat** Save your work surfaces by investing in a good-quality cutting mat. You will use this more than you might first think.
- **Craft scalpel** Ideal for cutting buttonholes or chopping through thicker materials, your craft scalpel is your friend!
- **Stitch picker/seam ripper** If you are working with recycled fabrics a lot (and if you take inspiration from this book, you undoubtedly will), then you will be glad these fellas are in your sewing box. Also a must-have for carrying out basic clothing alterations.

- **Dressmaker's pen** Another of my favourites. I prefer marking in pen than tailor's chalk, as I find it more precise and easier to use. Dressmaker's pen is special in that the ink is easily removable – don't ever substitute your sewing pen for a standard marker!
- **Ironing board and iron** Whether you have a designated iron and ironing surface or if you are using your domestic ones, you will come to find that you reach for your iron in almost all sewing projects. Keep them handy.

The Sewing Machine

Of course, one of the main pieces of equipment you need to get started with your new sewing schedule is a sewing machine. The mother of all time-saving sewing devices, your machine will become your buddy. The more time you spend with it, the better you will get to know it. The more comfortable you become in its company, the more you will achieve together! You needn't shell out large amounts of money on a fancy model. A good-quality, reliable machine with basic functions will do just fine. If you end up in the right place at the right time, you just might pick one up in your local charity shop for a tiny fraction of the price of a store-bought version. Before splashing your cash, ask around. I was amazed to find that my mother, who has never used a sewing machine in all her crafting years, had an old electric machine stashed away at the back of a cupboard. Left to her by my great aunt, the machine had been gathering dust for decades. Bingo! Also check out artists' studios and workshop complexes for potential bargains. When equipment is upgraded, the old machines need a home. You just might get lucky.

If you're not confident enough yet to tackle the set up of your machine, there is plenty of help available. The best starting point? A crafty pal who knows their way around a bobbin. If you are stuck for a sewing pro to help, there are some very helpful websites and You Tube videos that give step-by-step guides to getting yourself started with your new machine. Look 'em up. Or, if you are a complete beginner, why not seek out a local sewing class? Get to grips with the basics and then experiment to find your own ways of doing things.

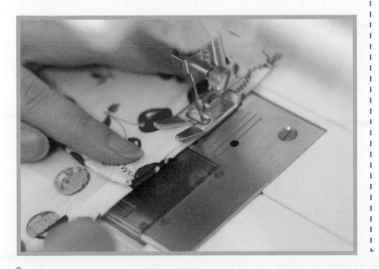

Basic Tools for Machine Sewing

- **Sewing machine** The variety of machines and the functions they perform is a brain boggler even for a seasoned sewer. To get started quickly and without huge investment, search out a basic, lightweight machine. As long as it has the capacity to run straight and zigzag stitches, you will manage fine.

- **Sewing machine needles** Just as with hand-sewing needles, pick up a pack that includes a variety of sizes. You might want to keep a jeans needle and a leather needle to hand too.

- **Bobbins** Start off with a collection of base colours – black, white, brown, grey and navy, then add others as your fabric stash and project list grows.

- **Presser foot** Your sewing machine will come with a standard presser foot but if you have managed to get your hands on a thrifted or reconditioned machine and the presser foot is missing, you can pick these up separately.

- **Zipper foot** If you are planning on sewing clothing and zip closures, then add one of these to your kit.

- **Small screwdriver** Most new store-bought sewing machines will come with an accessories kit included. The small screwdriver is key. Without it, you won't be able to change your needle and you won't be able to clean your machine properly.

- **Sewing machine oil** Your machine is a tough little blighter, but it does need care. A well kept, well cleaned and oiled machine will perform much better than a grimy neglected one and it will stand the test of time.

- **Small brush** This comes in handy for machine maintenance. A firm but tiny brush will allow you to sweep away dust and stray threads from the intricate innards of your machine.

MAKING TIME

If you are anything like me, your problem isn't so much deciding what to make in your craft time but in actually making time to craft. I have a list as long as my leg of projects I'd like to try and I have an even longer list of craft classes I'd like to join. However, running the Made in the Shade business takes up pretty much every waking hour of my life, leaving little time for anything else. How ironic then that the person that helps run the neo-craft business has

no time to craft! I guess I am lucky in that my job is firmly rooted in the craft scene and that my work incorporates all the creative strands I'm passionate about. Some busy girls aren't so fortunate …

So – between looking after a family, working all hours and trying to maintain some sort of social calendar, just when and how are you supposed to squish in the time to develop your sewing skills or actually complete a project?

Crafty Night In

Crafting should be something you enjoy in your fun time. It shouldn't feel like a chore. But, that said, the simplest way to make sure your creative side isn't neglected and lost in amongst the hubbub of everyday life is to formally schedule in some quality hours with your craft kit. Think of it like organizing a date to have an old friend round. In this scenario, the old friend is your sewing machine. Make a real occasion of craft time. Turn it into the point of the day, week or month where you really indulge yourself. Just picture the scene: you are wearing your comfiest slob-around clothes. You have a stack of great craft books and magazines within reach of one hand and a good supply of edible treats within reach of the other. For the next hour or two you have nothing else to think about but the latest project on your 'want to do' list. Sounds pretty good, huh? Your sewing machine will be so pleased to see you!

Sew on the Go!

One of the great things about sewing is that you can do it just about anywhere. Granted, it's not ideal to drag your sewing machine around with you. Neither is it customary to whip it out and plug it in in the waiting room of the opticians, but you could easily pop your current project in your handbag and hand stitch on the go whenever and wherever you get the chance. Your time is limited. Use it wisely and fill up spare bits with fun, crafty pursuits. Your train journey to work could be spent cross stitching; your lunch break spent embroidering; and the wait for the bus home from the supermarket? Surely best spent finishing off that last little embellishment!

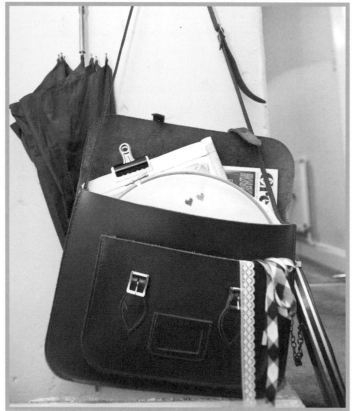

Hi-Ho, Hi-Ho
It's Off To Work We Go!

Making time to craft on a work day ...

- Once a week, leave for work an hour earlier than usual. Steal away some quiet stitching time in your favourite cafe en route. Ease into your busy day.
- Use tea breaks to browse your favourite crafty blog sites for inspiration or flip through a new craft book.
- Why not start up a sewing club in your workplace? Pick one day a week where you meet with colleagues at lunchtime to share ideas and tips.

Chunk!

Chunk It Up!

Sure, ideally it would be wonderful to sit down at your sewing machine and, without interruption, start a project and finish it in one great, long, glorious sewing session. It rarely happens that way though. For the busy girl, the key to a successful relationship with your sewing kit is this: chunking. Rather than get upset and frustrated that you just can't clear enough space in your diary to make that skirt or stitch up that cushion, you must rethink your strategy and redefine your goals. Work in chunks. You might not finish the skirt in one sitting, but in just one half-hour session you could prepare your fabric, take your measurements and cut out your waistband and skirt templates. Mission accomplished. Your next mission? To find a second half-hour session later in the week to pop in your box pleats. Mission accomplished. Your next mission? To find a third half-hour to ... You can see what I'm getting at. The projects in this book are organized into manageable little blocks of sewing activity. Get in the groove of working like this and you will be surprised at what you can achieve.

MAKING SPACE

People say that a tidy house makes for a tidy mind – although slightly prissy and a little bit 'Stepford', there's a lot to be said for that kind of thinking. To make a physical space for sewing helps to clear a mental space for sewing. Every girl needs a little hidey-hole – even if it's a pack-away hidey-hole. It doesn't matter whether your crafty nook is a specific section of your sofa, a tiny corner of your hallway or a vast dedicated studio space. The important thing is to make it your own. Set it up to look and function exactly as you want it to. Your sewing area needs to be a section of your home that you look forward to spending time in.

Compact Sense

Maybe right now you are surveying your apartment and feeling downhearted that you just can't section off a dedicated sewing studio. Don't be blue. If your home is compact and already full of crazy amounts of 'stuff' then you need to be resourceful. Maybe you don't have the room to set up a permanent craft station but try dedicating a cupboard or open shelving unit to your kit. Careful use of pretty boxes, crates, glass jars, vintage luggage and vanity cases make for a decorative display and functional, easily accessible storage. Until recently, my craft supplies were wheeled around on a hostess trolley!

Next time you are shopping in your local charity furniture store, look out for useful pieces. A gate-leg table, an ottoman, trolley, trunk, fold-away gaming table, bureau or vintage tall boy – all these items can be integrated cleverly into the decor of your home and make for great craft stowaways and desktops. With a little bit of loving care, junk furniture transforms into bespoke studio storage and workspace.

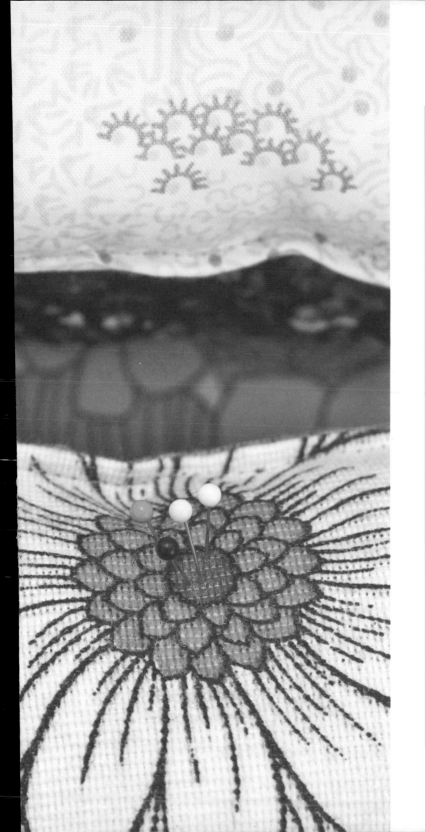

30 MINUTES OR LESS

Yes, you better believe it! These sewing projects, all designed by Made in the Shade gal, Clare Nicolson, will take no more than a sweet half hour of your precious time to complete. Simple and easy to digest, not only are they cute as a button, but every one is destined to become a well-used, much-loved addition to your growing craft kit. In between projects, relax and read a while. Have a nostalgic little rifle through my mother's sewing box, drool over my recent garage sale finds, then learn to tell your retro from your repro as we go trawling off the beaten track for interesting craft materials.

JUMBO PINCUSHION

by Made in the Shade

Next time you find yourself with half an hour to spare, spend it growing your craft kit – DIY style. This super-simple pincushion project is ideal for giving you a hit of crafty satisfaction in between checking off other items on your to-do list and is a useful (not to mention pretty) addition to your craft kit that you are sure to look back at fondly.

Project Notes

The Jumbo Pincushion is an easy project and one that even a novice like me completed quickly without too much drama. Not only did I find it an ideal practice project – perfect for getting a feel for machine sewing – but my impatient side was also kept at bay. Being able to start and finish a project in such a short space of time was really very satisfying. I heartily recommend you start here – and see where you end up! In the Stitch it up a Notch section at the close of the project, you'll find some ideas on how best to move forwards and build on the idea. Enjoy your adventure!

My talented friend and fellow Made in the Shader Clare Nicolson took up the role of sewing mistress during these 30-minute craft-a-long sessions. Get acquainted with Clare and with our creative ventures in the Getting To Know You feature at the end of the project.

Pleased as punch... ☑
Crafting calamity... ☐

Get ready to show off... ✿ your basic machine sewing skills

SEWING BOX ESSENTIALS

- ✿ 2 fabric pieces no smaller than 20cm (8in) square
- ✿ Knitting needle (or other long, thin, blunt object)
- ✿ Wadding (batting)
- ✿ Basic tool kit (see Getting Started)

1 Cut two pieces of fabric, each 20cm (8in) square and place on top of each other, patterned sides/ front sides facing.

2 Pin the fabric pieces together to secure them in place. The pins should be approximately 5cm (2in) apart.

Remember to remove your securing pins as you navigate round your square's edges. Don't get them caught up in your machine, or in your fingers. As a novice, I managed to prick my fingertips more than once!

3 Using your sewing machine, stitch a straight line around three sides of your fabric approximately 1cm (⅜in) from the edge, leaving the fourth edge open to create a little square pouch.

4 Using fabric scissors, snip the two stitched corners diagonally.

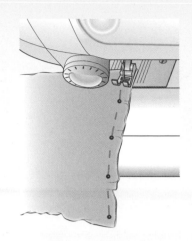

8 Go back to the sewing machine and stitch up the final open edge to seal up the pincushion, removing the pins as you stitch. Et voila!

5 Your pouch is currently inside out. Flip it round the right way and use an up-ended knitting needle or other long, thin, blunt object to push the corners out fully. Don't push too enthusiastically or you'll rip your lovely stitching.

This part can be quite fiddly. Push the wadding back a little bit to give you a better grip on the fabric edge. Don't worry though – you can always squish the stuffing back into position once you've stitched up the open edge.

6 Fill your pouch with wadding (batting) until it is nice and plump, leaving a gap of approximately 2cm (¾in) at the open side.

7 Take the fabric at the open side and fold it in on itself to form a neat edge and pin the edge in place.

Pin-Up Girls

Keen crafters are almost always equally keen collectors and incurable hoarders. If they're not rescuing usable fabric swatches from old clothes and storing stray buttons, they're rummaging around in bargain bins for trimmings and coloured threads. It doesn't take too long for the most paltry collection of craft supplies to multiply into a rather fine treasure trove of materials and tools.

Right now, as I start out on my journey to learn to sew, my stitching skills say, 'beginner' but my craft stash says, 'seasoned pro'. It's so much fun to collect things, either knowing you will use them, or just for collecting's sake. Pincushions are one of those cheeky little craft items that can mount up into an interesting collection pretty quickly. They're hard to resist! Perhaps this handmade one will be the beginning of a beautiful bunch ...

GETTING TO KNOW YOU: Clare Nicolson

Tool of choice: Sewing machine

Favourite artist: Collage artist, Sara Fanelli

Inspired by: Birds, nature and vintage ceramics, patterns, graphics and packaging

Most treasured possession: My vintage ceramic deer vase

Pet hates: Copycat designers and people being late!

Favourite food: Guacamole

Tip for growing your craft kit: Enjoy adding interesting things to your sewing box. Think beyond needles, threads and fabric squares; chopsticks are handy for poking out tricky edges, and net curtains make great lace-effect trims

GETTING TO KNOW YOU: Carrie Maclennan (that's me!)

Tool of choice: A notebook and pen

Crafting soundtrack: Old-time country music – Patsy Cline is a great working companion

Inspired by: Vintage fashion and lifestyle from the 40s and 50s, list making, paper, typography

Sewing aspirations: To make my own clothes and homewares

Pet hates: Liars, cheaters and double dealers

Favourite food: Mashed potatoes and tomatoes (not together)

Tip for growing your craft kit: Be thrifty and adventurous – dig a little deeper than your local craft megastore

STITCH IT UP A NOTCH

- This project can be easily adapted to produce other items. Try tinkering with full-sized cushion designs. When you feel it's time to try something a little more adventurous, experiment with embroidered or appliquéd motifs, button embellishments, trims or even patchwork.

- Next time you want to give a pal a quirky gift, try re-inventing the pattern as a cute miniature boudoir pillow. Incorporate delicate ribbon trims, vintage lace or frilled edging for a luxurious and feminine feel. Team pillows in sets of two or three, add a nostalgic old black-and-white photograph or a hand-picked selection of music and your handmade gift will stand out as super-special. Don't forget a beautiful handwritten label for that finishing touch.

- The Made in the Shade gals embrace 'granny chic' and love to incorporate old-time touches to fashion and home style. We've witnessed a resurgence in the popularity of lavender bags of late. If you wanted to, you could easily adapt the jumbo pincushion into an elegant drawer scent or pretty, scented vanity table accessory.

Stitching Up Nostalgia

Speak to any crafter about her early inspirations to pick up a needle and thread and nine times out of ten she will cite her mother, grandmother, aunt or other matriarchal figure as integral to her sewing story. As far back as I can remember, my mother has been knitting all kinds of woollen wearables and blankets for me and for the rest of my family. Over the years, she has fixed hems, sewn on buttons and reworked ill-fitting clothes as required. My mother and I share some crafty traits in that, like me, she will store clothes and textiles that need a little bit of love and care for months and months, fully intending to work her way through the pile, bringing old skirts and dresses back to life with a re-jigged hemline or a new zip. The difference between us? Unlike me, she does eventually make a start on her stack of 'will-dos'. When I was little, I wasn't particularly keen, or rather, I wasn't patient enough, to learn to knit or sew. However, lack of practical skills aside, I adored filing through my mother's knitting patterns, playing with her button box and staring into her basket of threads and measuring tapes.

Here are some of my favourite objects from my mother's sewing kit:

• **Knitting needle holder** I'm not entirely sure why, but I loved to push and pull the top of the holder on and off. I'd play with the needles inside – with a particular fascination with the size labels on the end!

• **Tupperware button box and needle keeper** This little tub is really nothing special. It started out as a kitchen item but over the years became the place where my mother stored all her tiny buttons. She would use the soft plastic lid as a needle holder, poking the points through into the tub to keep the sharp ends safe.

• **Wooden craft chest** Like a lot of ladies, my mother stores all her threads and sewing notions in a wooden craft chest. A hand-me-down item from a dear family member, this one replaced my mum's over-filled wicker sewing basket.

• **Button box** As a child I was never happier than when I was playing with my mum's button tin. I'd sort buttons according to colour, size and style. I loved just feeling all the tiny ones in my hands. Most children grow out of their fascination with buttons, but I never did. Despite having never sewn on a button until now, I have not just one tin of buttons in my house, but three. And the collection continues to grow.

Right now, you're building a craft kit to allow you to get going on that list of projects you've always wanted to try – but you might just be laying the foundation of someone else's sewing story too.

NATTY NEEDLECASE

by Made in the Shade

So, if the pins go in the pincushion – where do the needles go? In your needlecase! With the help of my partner in craft, Clare, we continue to stitch up a DIY craft kit. Whether sewing on the go or at home, this easy-to-make case will keep handy all the sharp little tools you need. Your needles will never end up stuck in the arm of the sofa or abandoned on surfaces again!

Project Notes

What's that? How did I get on with my needlecase project? Um. Yes. So I think I might need to improve my measuring and cutting-in-a-straight-line skills? My finished result is a little bit lopsided in places due to some squinty cutting. However, made from one of my favourite fabrics (it has 50s housewives on it), my needlecase is undoubtedly pretty, it's perfectly functional and it is now home to my needles. Just don't look too closely at my right angles! Despite the wonkiness? I am pleased as punch with my efforts. I'm guessing your results will be slightly more impressive than mine. Get to it!

With your needlecase complete, reward yourself a little light relief. Read fun titbits about designer Clare Nicolson's and my own wardrobe choices then pour a cup of tea and pick up hints on growing your sewing stash in the vintage shopping feature.

Pleased as punch... ☑

Crafting calamity... ☐

Get ready to show off... ❀ your basic measuring and cutting skills ❀ your basic machine sewing skills

SEWING BOX ESSENTIALS

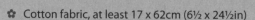

- 🌸 Cotton fabric, at least 17 x 62cm (6½ x 24½in)
- 🌸 2–4 felt sheets to tone with fabric, at least 13 x 28cm (5 x 11in)
- 🌸 Fusible interfacing
- 🌸 Pinking shears
- 🌸 Basic tool kit (see Getting Started)

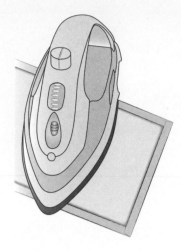

2 With your fabric still pattern-side down, iron the interfacing onto the reverse side. Then iron a 1cm (⅜in) fold around each side of the rectangle to secure in the interfacing and form a neat edge.

1 To make the outer cover of your case, lay your fabric pattern side down then mark out a rectangle measuring 17 x 62cm (6½ x 24½in) with dressmaker's pen or tailor's chalk. Cut it out. Then measure, mark and cut out an identical rectangle from the interfacing.

3 Fold the fabric in half lengthways and iron to make a crease down the centre of the fabric.

4 Using your sewing machine, stitch round all the edges with your favourite decorative stitch, approximately 1cm (⅜in) in from the edge.

These measurements might seem a little odd at first, but fret not! I promise you will end up with a cute needlecase measuring 15cm (6in) square by the final step.

Interfacing? What's Interfacing?

Interfacing is used to stiffen otherwise floppy fabrics. The cover of the needlecase will benefit from a little extra strength and rigidity. The interfacing we're using is 'fusible', which means it fuses to the fabric with a special heat-activated adhesive – all we have to do is iron it on! There are various types and weights of interfacing available – if you are unsure which kind you need to use with a particular fabric, ask the advice of your local haberdasher before investing.

I'm a big fan of decorative stitches – even though the machine is doing all the creative sewing for me, I somehow feel like I am sewing 'more' if I use a zigzag or scalloped pattern!

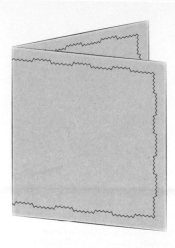

5 Fold your fabric in half again then iron to make a neat crease in the centre fold. You have made the pretty cover of your needlecase!

6 Now you need to make the pages. Cut your coloured felt sheets into rectangles measuring 13 x 28cm (5 x 11in). Use pinking shears to give a decorative edge and super-cute finish. Cut however many pages you like – two to four felt sheets is ideal, making four to eight pages.

Quick Finder File

To help differentiate between types of needles and to make it easier to flip to the one you need quickly, cut your pages to different sizes to make a sort of felt needle 'file'.

7 Fold the book of felt pages in half and press down firmly to mark the centre crease. Open the book up again and position the felt sheets together neatly in the centre of the needlecase cover and pin in place.

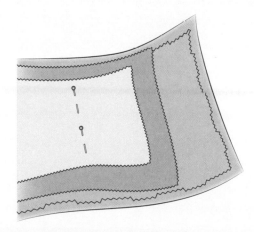

8 Using your sewing machine, sew down the centre crease of your case with a straight stitch, securing the pages in place. Close over your needlecase then iron to crisp up the spine. Now – go and find those stray needles and pop them in their place!

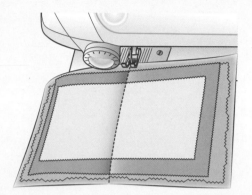

Turning a Corner
Rather than repeatedly lifting your needle and presser foot to re-angle your fabric, when turning a corner leave your needle in the fabric (to keep it in place). Lift the presser foot with the needle still in position then rotate your fabric as desired. Perfect corners every time!

Practice Makes Perfect

Get to know your sewing machine. Spend some time simply sewing in straight lines over and over again to get a feel for the machine and to build your sewing confidence. When I first switched my trusty sewing buddy on, I would jerk and jump at the slightest blip! With some practice though, judders and funny noises come and go and sewing continues uninterrupted!

Even the most basic machine will have a few stitch choices to experiment with. For example, my machine has three decorative stitches and multiple zigzag options. With fabric remnants at hand, try out each setting on your machine and see what results you can achieve. Think about the projects you have on your 'to do' list. You might happen upon the perfect decorative stitch to add interest to your needlecase, or you might want to think about stitching a fancy hem into your duvet skirt (see chapter 3)?

For the beginner, machine sewing with a decorative stitch is rather exciting! I somehow feel like I'm sewing 'more' if I use a decorative stitch rather than a straight stitch. Not only can I achieve some pretty finishes on my work without really trying too hard, but a decorative stitch can help hide a multitude of sins if, like me, your sewing-in-a-straight-line skills have yet to be honed!

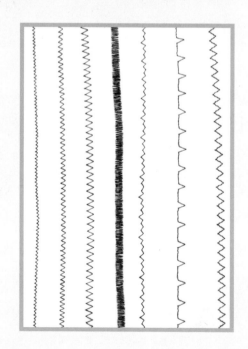

TRADEMARK STYLE: Carrie

"Carrie looks like a wee girl but she dresses like a granny"
Garry (Carrie's husband)

Less rockabilly pin-up and more 1950s square, I guess I like to mash up all manner of retro styles from the 1940s and 50s. I try for Natalie Wood à la *Rebel Without A Cause* but sometimes end up looking more like Joany from *Happy Days* via granny chic jumble! I love to be cosy and comfortable. I own more cardigans and woollen items than anyone I know.

Style icons: Bettie Page, Debbie Reynolds
Favourite wardrobe item: My red patent wedges or vintage Japanese clogs. Oh! Or my tweed, fur-cuffed coat.
Fashion bugbears: Neon, wearing sunglasses indoors

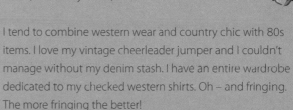

TRADEMARK STYLE: Clare

"Clare dresses the way The Pink Ladies would in the 60s. And sometimes a bit like a Golden Girl!"
John (Clare's boyfriend)

I tend to combine western wear and country chic with 80s items. I love my vintage cheerleader jumper and I couldn't manage without my denim stash. I have an entire wardrobe dedicated to my checked western shirts. Oh – and fringing. The more fringing the better!

Style icons: Bianca Jagger, Zooey Deschanel
Favourite wardrobe item: The leather belt I bought in Texas – or my high waisters
Fashion bugbears: Ugg boots, wearing too many animal prints at once

STITCH IT UP A NOTCH

- Instead of using felt to make your needlecase pages, dig through your scraps of vintage fabrics. Stitch two patterned pieces together back to back to create a busy, double-sided floral page.

- Get handy with decorating the cover of your case. Hand embroider a line from your favourite song or stitch in a motivational crafty slogan!

- Embellish your case. There's always scope for a ribbon or lace trim round the outer edge.

Shop 'til You Drop: Sourcing Secondhand Supplies

Every busy girl needs a break – and what better way to justify a day out than to insist that it's positively essential to your crafty wellbeing. Heck – if you didn't take the odd opportunity to 'shop it up' now and again, your creative urges would surely be suppressed and eventually, your brain might just pop. And then where would you be? Throw caution to the wind, scrub your schedule clean of all appointments and chores and hit the town for a day of supplies shopping.

Craft ♥s Vintage

At first, it might seem unusual to find yourself reading an article about vintage shopping in a sewing book. Think again. The relationship between the craft community and vintage/secondhand shopping is a close one. Sharing a lot in common, craft and vintage are often seen hanging out together at craft fairs, in shops and even out on the street in the outfits of indie shoppers. The two complement each other and work well together – aesthetically and philosophically. They do make a handsome couple.

The crafter creates tangible 'things' – decorative objects, useful items, clothing, homewares – while the vintage shopper creates a fresh perspective, an imaginative and unique 'style' by breathing new life into used goods and combining pieces from different fashion schools and eras. Boredom is a major motivator for busy girls to make things. Bored with the homogeneity of the high street and with a desire to reclaim and create some smidgeon of difference, she starts crafting up her own designs, carving out her own little niche. The very same motivation exists for the vintage shopper. Why construct a style or visual identity using the same tools and components as everyone else? She searches beyond the mall and chooses to shake up the chain-store trend – stomping on it a little bit as she swooshes off in her secondhand coat!

Before You Set Off ...

- **Wear comfy shoes** There is nothing more disappointing than having to cut a shopping jaunt short because your tootsies give in before you do.

- **Bag a banana** Thrifting is energetic work. Fill your pockets with some emergency provisions.

- **Set a budget** Try to be disciplined and don't fritter away your pocket money. Cap spending and be sure to stick to your agreed limit!

- **Plan your route** Don't waste precious time darting round town blindly from store to store. Plot a sensible trail.

- **Call for back up** Drag a chum along for support. You need someone to rein you in when faced with a particularly tempting potential budget blower. And, when you're struggling to carry your craft haul home, you have someone to lend a hand!

Reuse and Repurpose

Whether shopping secondhand out of necessity or making and mending for fun, the two go hand in hand. The added bonus being that, for the crafty type, the secondhand buy from the charity shop will later be lovingly reconstructed and cleverly customized, resulting in an as-new, stand-out style statement. Indeed, over time, the vintage shopper may find that she needs to get handy with a needle and thread if she wants to fix that loose hem or stitch a patch over that little hole in her new vintage blouse. The new-wave craft scene celebrates the reusing and 'upcycling' of found and forgotten objects and materials. A vintage napkin becomes a hanging tree, a forgotten 45 becomes a knick-knacks dish, an old duvet cover becomes a skirt, an old brooch becomes a necklace, a 1970s apron is revived, a lost button takes pride of place on a piece of wall art … you get the idea. Nothing goes to waste and those 'want not' items that usually end up in the trash are rescued and made new again.

Every item the crafty girl makes with her own fair hand has a story that no mass-produced product will ever have. Her finished product has a homespun tale to tell before it has even hit the shelf of her local indie boutique. It's a story worth telling and one that customers want to learn about and contribute to. Similarly, the vintage shopper will pluck out those special pieces from the rest. Respectful of their durability, quality and craftsmanship, she is thrilled that they are well-preserved enough for her to enjoy them and delighted that she will add to their already rich life story.

There are guys and gals out there immersed in the vintage and craft 'scenes' (if we want to call them that) who would likely describe their engagement as a lifestyle – as going beyond just shopping habits or crafty hobbies. Reminiscent of the spirit of 1940s wartime rationing or the heyday of the WI, they are perpetually and instinctively making and mending, making do and reusing. More than just a means to buck high-street fashion trends, they combine a passion for the old with a desire to create something exciting and it seeps into everything they do. Inspired by old-time values and cultural reference points, sometimes with a political agenda, sometimes not, these folks are diamonds in the rough of 'same old same old'. Part granny-chic, part rock 'n' roll maverick, you will, more often than not, find these active souls somewhere at the heart of the most interesting and vibrant craft scenes and, to me at least, they are truly inspirational.

Vintage

Both Clare and I have been secondhand thrifters and vintage shoppers since our early teens. I prefer to invest in vintage fashion for numerous reasons, the first being, simply, that I have a passion for the style of a particular era. I want to buy into a little piece of style from the 1940s and 50s. I love the fact that pre-owned garments have their own biographies. However, authentic garments often come with hefty price tags that reflect the quality, condition and back-story of the item. I view genuine vintage products in the same way someone else might view a designer label – as covetable, as aspirational and as something special to be saved up for!

Retro

Fashion and homestyle always harks back to other decades for inspiration and I am lucky in that my favourite styles of the 40s and 50s have popped up to shape trends in the 80s, in the 90s and are >

< influencing high-street collections even now. A cheaper alternative to buying genuine pieces is to seek out a 40s-style tea dress made for a chain store in the 80s or to buy a pair of 50s-style peep-toe wedges from the high street.

Repro

An increasing interest in vintage fashion and lifestyle has given rise to a number of niche designers and dressmakers who reproduce vintage patterns, or design and make new pieces heavily inspired by the original pattern. I adore reproduction vintage, as I find it very difficult to find genuine 40s and 50s pieces to fit. This way, I can have my dream frock and needn't worry too much about having to get trussed up just to fit into the bodice! I can purchase reproduction utility denim and 40s-style suits as easily as I could totter round my local mall. Repro combines my love of handmade with my love of vintage. Perfect!

Secondhand

Secondhand shopping has recently enjoyed a huge resurgence. Shopping secondhand was once seen as something that was done out of necessity – not for pleasure or preference. Now though, secondhand stores are frequented by an astonishingly wide customer base – different segments of which having different motivations for shopping there.

When I bang on about my love for vintage style, I'm sometimes met with scoffs and rolling eyes. 'Phht, vintage? It used to be called secondhand in my day.' Yes. With the exception of rare 'never sold' warehouse finds, all vintage items are secondhand (pre-owned). However – not all secondhand items are vintage! This is the key. Broadly, I would consider pre-1980s items to be vintage and pre-1920s to be antique. Secondhand items can be as little as just a few days or weeks old. This isn't to say that you won't uncover some vintage gems in the secondhand shop though – and you probably won't be asked to pay vintage store prices for them either.

Growing Your Sewing Stash
Keep your peepers peeled for …

Clothes

Trawl charity shops and high-street sales for bargain fabrics. Ignore the style of the garment and concentrate on identifying appealing patterns, colours, textures and weights. The womenswear and children's departments will be crammed full of retro florals, geometric designs and cute pastels but don't bypass the menswear section – you might miss out on some great tweeds, plaids and denims. Your local vintage store is a great source for scarves – ideal for repurposing.

Curtains

My fabric bundle isn't short of a vintage curtain length or two. Buying up stock of cheap secondhand or mid-price vintage curtains is an inexpensive way to get your hands on high-quality, heavyweight fabrics for interior projects and wearables. Put them in your basket! Net curtains get a bad press these days, shunned by interior designers and mocked by the style police. I adore them. Think twice before leaving them behind in the bargain bin. Dye those babies up in super-vivid colours and you open up a whole new world of textile design opportunities!

Table linens

Apart from their obvious potential for use as good-sized linen remnants, vintage tablecloth embroidery details can be rescued and reused too. Also look out for lace doilies, runners and fabric place mats for use in smaller projects.

Bed linens

With just a little bit of seam picking and a trim here and there, duvet covers and pillowcases offer a cost-effective alternative to store-bought cottons. Dig around to find wonderful patterns and finishes.

Project inspirations

Remember – your search for crafty supplies is not limited to materials and fixings. Dressmaking patterns have become a staple find at the best vintage fairs and ask in your local secondhand book store if they have any old 'how-to' craft guides lurking in a box somewhere. If you can find a good stockist, vintage magazines are loaded with inspiration too and old housekeeping and lifestyle weeklies can be fun sources for quirky projects just waiting to be brought up to date with a cheeky twist. Don't limit yourself to craft publications for new ideas. Antique photo albums, style books and beautifully illustrated children's stories are just some of the sources I like to keep handy. Pick up a bundle at antique markets and jumble sales.

Craft nook additions

On your journey, keep a look out for pretty things to spruce up your craft area. Think of them, not just as decorative items, but as an extension of your ideas board. Everything in your craft nook should excite, motivate and inspire you. Vintage teacups make unusual pots for small plants. Pick up old crockery items and compartmentalized serving dishes to use as desk tidies. Tins, boxes and baskets never go amiss in a craft nook and vintage suitcases and trunks make ideal stores for fabrics and items you don't need access to all the time. Odd ceramic figurines, vases and knick-knacks add an extra splash of eye candy on your supplies shelf. Retro household items such as wooden laundry airers and vegetable racks can be repurposed in your craft room too. Store yarns, threads and larger supplies in tiered baskets or use the airer to store and display freshly ironed fabric lengths.

Geek Chic

I grew up in a house where hand-me-downs and handmades were put to best use. My mother, never one to follow trends or fads, would rarely – if ever – succumb to my pleas for the latest this or the latest that. In response to my pre-adolescent whining, she would simply say, 'That? No. Common as muck'. She prioritized practicality, quality and value over fashion and didn't allow a single designer label to creep into my wardrobe. Growing up, I didn't always appreciate being the geeky kid with the hand-knitted jumpers and the utilitarian coat and shoes. In fact, at times, I hated it. At other times though, I secretly loved my so-called unfashionable clothes (but pretended otherwise to my school friends to save face). In hindsight, had my mother not steered me clear from fly-by-night fads, encouraging me instead to experiment with thrifty style alternatives and to celebrate difference – goodness only knows how I would have turned out. I'd never really considered it until now, but my mum is the original forward-thinking thrifter! Thanks to her, here I am, flying the DIY flag and championing the fabulousness of the charity shop and vintage store.

WELL-DRESSED NOTEBOOK

by Made in the Shade

I have quite the penchant for notebooks. I keep one for every purpose. Lists, notes, ideas, contacts, craft tips – they each have their own designated book. While you might not be quite so particular, it's always a good idea to keep a journal to hold all your project inspirations, to-do lists and tips in one place. Let's run with the DIY craft kit theme and spruce up your sewing notes with this easy-to-make book cover.

Project Notes

OK, OK, so my finished result is a bit wonky – but I'm not ticking the crafting calamity box just yet! My stitching is a little squint making for a neat fit in places, and my idea of 'straight' maybe isn't the same as everyone else's, but I am pleased as punch with my new notebook cover. Clare advised I use a scalloped stitch. In hindsight I don't think she was making a merely aesthetic recommendation. My chosen stitch helped hide a multitude of sins! Practice makes perfect, and I do have a lot of notebooks to cover ...

Clare usually spends her time whipping up beautiful interiors pieces, but she put these projects together with the busy girl in mind. She was particularly excited to help me make my own book cover. She knew how excited I would be to dress up my stationery!

Pleased as punch... ☑
Crafting calamity... ☐

Get ready to show off... ❀ your basic measuring and cutting skills ❀ your basic machine sewing skills

SEWING BOX ESSENTIALS

❀ Hardback notebook
❀ Fabric (size dependent on book, see steps 1–2)
❀ Basic tool kit (see Getting Started)

1 To calculate the width of the fabric, measure the width of your notebook and multiply the measurement by two. Measure the spine of the book, add this to the previous figure then add 22cm (8½in).

2 To calculate the length of the fabric required, measure the height of your notebook then add 6cm (2½in).

3 Place your fabric flat, pattern-side down, on the work surface and measure and mark your dimensions using tailor's chalk or a dressmaker's pen. Cut out the rectangle of fabric.

4 Keeping your fabric pattern side down, fold in 1cm (⅜in) along each edge of your fabric and iron the folds. To ensure a nice neat finish, iron the folds along both the long sides first, then both the short sides.

5 Using a pretty decorative stitch and toning thread, sew straight along the short sides, 0.5–1cm (⅛–⅜in) from the edge.

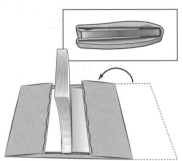

6 Place your fabric pattern side down again and position your notebook on top. Wrap the fabric around the cover of your book. Fiddle around with the fabric a little bit until you have equal-sized folds inside the front and back covers.

7 Once you are satisfied that your folds are roughly the same size, iron gently then pin them in place.

Open and Shut

Close the book to allow you to make sure you've got the right seam allowance and to make sure the size of the spine has been accommodated. You need to make sure that with its new cover on, your notebook still opens and closes properly.

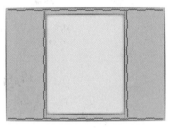

8 Using the same decorative stitch as in step 5, sew along both long sides of the cover, stitching the folds in place as you go.

9 Iron to create a neat finish, then slip your notebook into its new cover (see tip, below).

Dress Your Notebook

To insert your notebook into its cover, open the book and flip back the front and back hard covers so they meet back to back. Open your fabric cover and flip back both the front and back of that too. Slide your book into your book cover. Close your book – et voila!

WHO LIVES IN A MAISONETTE LIKE THIS?

The Maisonette, or 'little home' is our retail space dedicated to showcasing and selling handmade work by super-talented designer-makers. Working with a network of around 40 makers at any one time, we work our bobby socks off to promote handmade products – and the clever hands and minds that create them. We stock everything from ceramics and textile homewares to books and stationery.

The Maisonette is built and styled entirely with secondhand, found, restored or repurposed furniture. This wardrobe was bought from a charity shop and painted up pretty by our own fair hands to become our 'office'. We keep everything we need for running the shop behind this door. The 1950s kitchen larder is our packing station.

With nothing but a couple of sheets of MDF, a hinge or two and some blackboard paint, Clare whipped up our A-frame all by herself. She added The Maisonette logo by papercutting a stencil and filling it in with chalk. Isn't she clever?

Some businesses brighten up their workspaces with pot plants and blooms. We collect cacti. Lots of 'em. A big prickly cactus adds a dash of greenery to your surroundings and you don't have to spend hours tending to it – perfect for a busy girl.

STITCH IT UP A NOTCH

- As an extra little flourish, sew a length of ribbon around the outside of your cover. Leave two loose lengths at the open edge of your book. Tie your ideas safely in a bow when you're not scribbling secret plans!

- It's no use having a fabulous notebook if you've got nothing to write in it with. By adding a small ribbon or fabric loop, you could make a simple holder for your favourite pen too.

- Take the book cover out of the craft room and into the kitchen. Stitch up a book cover made from wipe-clean oilcloth and use it to cover your recipe journal. There are some amazing patterned oilcloth fabrics available from your local haberdasher.

- Adapt the measurements to accommodate ring binders and files. There ain't nothing you can't cover!

KEEP-IT-NEAT PATTERN SLEEVE

by Made in the Shade

Storing patterns and project notes in ring binders is a good idea, but if you're sewing on the go or collecting inspiration for your next crafty endeavour, then this DIY pattern sleeve could become one of your most-used craft kit items. Keep all the bits you need for your current project, or snippets and swatches for your next project, safe in this simple yet beautiful fabric folder.

Project Notes

I think the pattern sleeve project is my very favourite one in this chapter. A relatively drama-free session sewing session by my standards, I had a fun time making my pretty pouch. Quick and easy to make, I absolutely love the version I made from old curtain fabric. I was also delighted to find that my trusty laptop slid into my sleeve perfectly!

Pleased as punch... ☑

Crafting calamity... ☐

Clare and I had such a fun time working through this project. By the time I worked up to making my sleeve, I felt much more comfortable with the sewing machine and was able to 'go it alone' a little more than I had before!

Get ready to show off... ✿ your basic measuring and cutting skills
✿ your basic machine sewing skills

SEWING BOX ESSENTIALS

- ✿ Fabric, at least 140 x 40cm (55 x 15¾in)
- ✿ Long, thin, blunt object (up-ended knitting needle or chopstick)
- ✿ A4 paper/book/magazine (as template/ size checker)
- ✿ Pretty button
- ✿ Basic tool kit (see Getting Started)

1 Choose and iron your fabric. Pick a strong material with a fabulous pattern – an old curtain maybe? Make sure you adore your fabric. You'll be using your pattern sleeve a lot!

2 Fold the fabric in half pattern side to pattern side, measure and mark a 70 x 40cm (27½ x 15¾in) rectangle using dressmaker's pen. Still keeping the fabric doubled, cut out the shape with fabric scissors and pin the two rectangles together neatly. Alternatively, if you want a contrasting fabric on the inside of your sleeve, cut two rectangles from different fabrics and pin together pattern side to pattern side.

3 Using your sewing machine set to a plain stitch, sew along the two longest sides 1cm (⅜in) from the edge. Then, sew along just one of the shorter sides, leaving the other open.

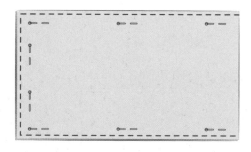

4 With fabric scissors, snip off the excess fabric at the two sewn edges in a neat diagonal.

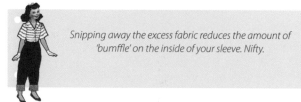

Snipping away the excess fabric reduces the amount of 'bumffle' on the inside of your sleeve. Nifty.

5 Turn your rectangle right side out so that the pattern side is now on the outside. Use a long, thin, blunt object (up-ended knitting needle, chopstick or similar) to help turn out the corners.

6 Iron the rectangle so that the new seams are crisp. Then, take the remaining open side of your rectangle and fold it in on itself to make a neat, straight edge. Iron flat to secure then pin in place.

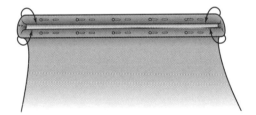

7 Using your sewing machine, this time set to your favourite decorative stitch, sew up the remaining open side about 1.5cm (½in) (or as close as possible) from the edge.

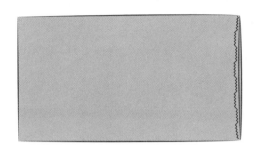

8 Take a piece of A4 paper or a magazine and place it onto what would be the middle third of your rectangle, as a template guide to decide where your sleeve folds should be.

9 Fold up the bottom third of the sleeve until the short edge reaches the top of the template. Next, fold down the top third to create a flap. Fiddle around with the positioning of the template to decide where you want the edge of your flap to sit when the sleeve is buttoned closed.

In the end, my sleeve flap lay around 3–4cm (1–1½in) from the bottom of my sleeve. This seemed to work well.

10 Iron the folds in place, then pin the bottom piece in place and open up the flap. Using your favourite decorative stitch, sew down both long sides of your sleeve – from the top of your flap to the bottom around 1cm (⅜in) from the edge. With the same stitch, sew along the top edge of the flap to create a pretty finishing touch.

11 Choose a favourite button from your collection. Measure the width of the button then add on 5mm (⅛in). This final measurement will be the required width of the buttonhole.

12 Measure the width of the flap edge, find the centre point and mark with a pin.

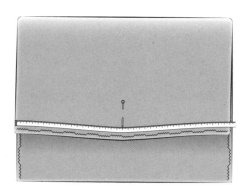

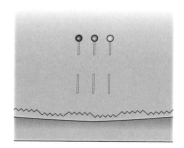

13 Mark where the buttonhole will be positioned on the flap. To make sure your buttonhole is in the centre of your flap, divide the required width of the buttonhole by two and then mark that measurement on either side of the pin with two more pins.

Don't be scared by all these sums! It's easy peasy. My button measured 2cm (¾in). With the extra 5mm (¼in) added, the final width of my buttonhole was 2.5cm (1in). Having then divided this by two, I marked 1.25cm (½in) on either side of my marker pin.

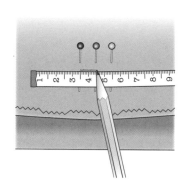

14 Decide how far up on your flap you want your button to sit. With dressmaker's pen, draw a guide line for your buttonhole using the pins to position your buttonhole in the centre of your sleeve flap.

15 Using your sewing machine, make a buttonhole using the pen line as a guide for the length. Each machine will have its own special setting to make buttonholes. If you are unsure whether you machine has the setting or if you need help using it, refer to your instruction manual for guidance.

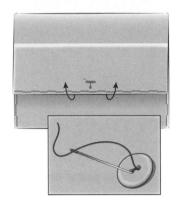

Button Up

If you find that your machine doesn't have an automated buttonhole function, fret not! You can make your buttonhole with your own fair hand and trusty needle and thread.

1. Using either sharp sewing scissors or a craft knife, cut a line through the pen mark guide line.
2. Thread your needle with strong thread. Choose toning thread to disguise the buttonhole, or make a feature of it by using bright, contrasting thread. Doubling or quadrupling up the thread is recommended to help band up the buttonhole more quickly and more effectively.
3. Start stitching your buttonhole around 2mm (1⁄16in) from the edge. Keep wrapping the threads until the entire buttonhole is securely banded up round the edges.

---

17 With your flap closed, mark the centre point of the buttonhole with a pin positioned upright, poking out of the buttonhole. Gently open the flap, keeping the marker pin in place. Using the pin as a starting point, sew your button in place.

18 With the sleeve closed, iron the entire sleeve, then fill it up with your patterns, project ideas and paper scraps!

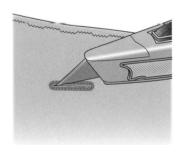

16 Once your machine has worked its buttonhole magic, take your craft knife or sewing scissors and cut down the centre of the buttonhole, right through the fabric.

JUST THE TWO OF US …

Clare and I make the perfect pair to run a business. Our strengths are well matched and we balance out each other's weaknesses. Clare is the upbeat, sunny-sider while I am the 'what-if'er. I am the wordy one, while she is the artistic one. We come up with ideas together – our brains are in sync!

Clare

'I create all our business branding and undertake all design work. If it's not pretty and it doesn't involve graph paper, I'm not interested! I work in The Maisonette and take care of the shop displays, stock choices and designer liaison. You can find me blogging about my obsession with typography and my love of pattern every week on the Made in the Shade blog. I'm also the business's bookkeeper and sum-doer. Zzzzz'.

Carrie

'Where there's writing to be done for the business – web copy, blog, press work, customer mail-outs and so on – you will find me nearby typing frantically. I'm also the obsessive list maker, compulsive double checker and general worry wart. When I'm not posting pretty parcels to our online shop customers, I write for the Made in the Shade Digest and make links on our many social networking sites.'

STITCH IT UP A NOTCH

- Instead of using ordinary fabric for your pattern sleeve, try using cross stitch Aida fabric. If you are feeling adventurous, cross stitch patterns, emblems, slogans, or even a lovely stylized version of your name onto your sleeve.

- Add a foam innard between your fabric pieces to make a protective laptop sleeve.

- Sandwich a good quality, heavy interfacing between the two fabric pieces and play with the dimensions of the sleeve to make a basic clutch bag.

- Follow steps 1 to 6 to make the basis of a comfy pillow for your craft chair. Insert a pillow or fill with wadding as desired then simply stitch up the remaining open end.

Garage Sale Show & Tell

Always on the look out for vintage treasure and usable crafty bits, the Made in the Shade gals do love a good garage sale. As the saying goes, one person's tat is another person's treasure. Take yourself out to car-boot sales, street markets and garage sales and get rummaging. You never can predict the fabulous items you might unearth in boxes of someone else's cast-offs. Here are some of my favourite thrifty finds ...

Bundle of vintage table linens and lace
I did mean to use some of these fabrics as they were intended, but they have since joined my craft kit for use in all the sewing projects I will get round to once I've practised. This tablecloth is my favourite of the bundle.

Big bag o' ribbons
Green Is my very favourite colour. Everywhere I go I seek out green things. I purchased a bag of ribbons because these smashers grabbed my attention.

Big bag o' buttons
I can spy a pretty button from 50 paces. It was hard to miss this whopper among the crowd. Sold!

Box of embroidery threads
I couldn't believe my eyes! There it was – I had to have it. These are just some of the rainbow of threads I found inside.

ONE HOUR OR LESS

These interiors, wearables and accessories projects will slot neatly into your scheduled sewing hour. Taking a measly 60 minutes – or even less – to complete, turn your hand to basic embellishment, cross stitch, embroidery and quilting techniques. Just as exciting, you will meet the super-talented designer-makers that kindly contributed their designs for you to try, and will learn a little about them, their passions and their inspirations. In this chapter, feature articles take a sociable approach to crafting. We join the online craft community and get to grips with blogging and forum etiquette, then we get ready to host a crafty party at home.

HAPPY HOOPY WALL ART

by Rachael Lamb

If you're anything like me you'll have an enormous stash of fabric remnants, buttons and pretty charms that you promise you will one day transform into beautiful adornments for your home. But do you ever get round to it? With these wonderfully simple wall art pieces, there's no excuse. With the most basic of sewing skills you can whip up a collection of these with your eyes shut, but peepers will pop when your visitors see them! Low effort – high impact. Perfect!

Project Notes

There were a few hairy moments in my stitch-a-long session where I feared that I might make a crafting calamity of perhaps the simplest project in this book! However, with a little assistance from the lovely Rachael my hoop wall art turned out beautifully. If I ever grumble again about not having time to make home accessories, I give y'all full permission to open this book, at this page, and poke me with a needle until I get my embroidery hoops and button jar out!

Pleased as punch... ☑

Crafting calamity... ☐

Crafty business owner Rachael Lamb was my sewing guide in this project. The lesson took place at her shop, Hannah Zakari, which is so full of beautiful objects it was hard to concentrate on my stitching! Learn more about Rachael and what makes her tick in the Meet the Maker section at the end of the project.

Get ready to show off... ✿ your imagination ✿ your eye for detail ✿ your basic hand sewing skills

SEWING BOX ESSENTIALS

❀ Wooden embroidery hoop(s)
❀ Pretty fabric(s) to fit the hoop(s)
❀ Selection of buttons
❀ Basic tool kit (see Getting Started)

1 Dig out all those lengths of fabric that have piled up high in your craft basket. Select a piece to use as a base for your wall art. Give it a quick iron to remove any creases.

2 Cut a piece of fabric around 6cm (2in) larger than your embroidery hoop and place it on top of the inner hoop.

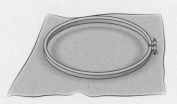

3 Carefully place the outer hoop, over the top. Tighten up the screw on the hoop to make sure your fabric stays taught. If after screwing your hoops together you find your fabric is still a little flabby, pull it tight.

4 Rake through your button collection for pretties that look nice on the chosen fabric – selecting them by shape, colour or theme. Place all your 'shortlisted' buttons onto the work surface. Spend some time experimenting with different button combinations and arrangements.

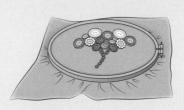

5 Artfully arrange the embellishments in a pretty pattern on the fabric. Once you have landed on your perfect set, slide the formation off the fabric and begin sewing the buttons on in order, one by one.

Arranging the buttons artfully might sound easy, but it's actually quite tricky! Do you want your flourish of buttons to meet the edge of the hoop? Top or bottom? Jaunty and freeform or straight and linear? Decisions, decisions … Take your time over this part, try out lots of different combinations and positions before settling on the final arrangement.

Beginner Buttons
If you are a total novice you might find it easier to use buttons with exposed holes rather than ones with the hole concealed on the underside.

Horizontal to Vertical
The hoop will eventually be hung up, so think about this when stitching – if you have chosen buttons that wobble around rather than lie flat, prop them up with other embellishments so that you don't have any droopy sections when the hoop is hanging on your wall.

6 Once you have finished sewing on your buttons, check that the fabric is still taught. If it has become loose, gently pull the fabric around the hoop by hand to tighten it again.

7 Carefully cut off the excess fabric to the size of the hoop. You are now ready to hang your hoop proudly. Or you are ready to stitch hundreds more to cover an entire wall!

MEET THE MAKER: Rachael Lamb

Rachael Lamb is an indie design high flyer. Her boutique, Hannah Zakari, is a one-stop shop for the best in handmade work and exciting design pieces. With a keen eye for the little details and for all things beautiful, Rachael also produces her own range of bags and jewellery. Her heart begins a-fluttering at the sight of a glorious fabric pattern and in this project, she shows off her innate ability to create something wonderful from mere remnants and odds and ends.

Tool of choice: Needle and thread

Most treasured possession: My red Vivienne Westwood shoes

Favourite food: A nice juicy beefburger

Favourite artist: Right now, I love Japanese artist Naoshi

Inspired by: The artefacts and the materials I work with – fabric, patterns, beads and buttons

Crafting soundtrack: I'm a 90s indie chick – Pulp, Blur and Super Furry Animals

Favourite jam: Berries – not just strawberry, not just raspberry, but lots and lots of different berries!

STITCH IT UP A NOTCH

- Why stop at buttons for embellishment? Put broken jewellery and found charms to good use and incorporate them into your designs.

- Since you're making art from an embroidery hoop, embrace it! Hand embroider messages, shapes or patterns onto your fabric before adding further 3D embellishments.

- Pick a fabric with an illustrated print then recreate the pattern on top in coloured sequins and other sparkly bits to create a fancy mosaic effect.

THE HANGING TREE

by Wooden Tree

Wooden Tree is the pseudonym of textile artist Kirsty Anderson. For this hanging fabric ornament, she has adapted one of her trademark designs especially with busy crafters in mind. Intended to add a beautiful and much-needed calming feature to your home or workspace, This is a beautifully simple project, and as you will see from the Stitch It Up a Notch section at the end of the chapter, it is easily adaptable and customizable too.

Project Notes

I am thrilled to have completed Kirsty's Hanging Tree project successfully. Made from a vintage napkin once belonging to former Made in the Shade colleague Suzanne Smith, my tree is loaded with sentimental value and will now serve as a reminder of a fantastic friendship, as well as being testament to my burgeoning sewing machine skills!

This project is designed by nimble-fingered crafty lady Kirsty Anderson. As well as teaching me to sew the tree, Kirsty also arranged a little tea party – complete with home baking and vintage crockery! Discover more about Kirsty's influences at the end of the project.

Pleased as punch... ☑
Crafting calamity... ☐

Get ready to show off...   ✿ those nimble fingers   ✿ your basic machine sewing skills
✿ your basic hand sewing skills

SEWING BOX ESSENTIALS

✿ Fabric remnants
✿ Tracing paper
✿ Pencil and ruler
✿ Narrow ribbon
✿ Knitting needle (or other long, thin, blunt object)
✿ Wadding (batting)
✿ Basic tool kit (see Getting Started)

1 First, choose your fabric. Rather than invest in a heap of new material from the haberdasher, why not challenge yourself to find suitable scraps within your existing collection?

Fabric Choice

These trees look beautiful in plain or patterned fabric – stick to one block of colour or choose a pretty vintage floral. For an extra-special finish, search for self-coloured fabrics adorned with delicate printed or embroidered motifs. Old pillowcases or napkins work well. Try combining colours and patterns, perhaps using different but complementary fabrics for the front and reverse.

2 Lay the tracing paper over the tree template (see Templates) and trace around the shape with your pencil and ruler then cut out the shape to make your template.

Template Tip

Use tracing paper to make your tree template. You can use card or regular paper, but you will be thankful for a semi-transparent template. You'll be able to see the design of your fabric through the tracing paper, allowing you to 'frame' your tree perfectly.

3 Place the tracing paper template onto the fabric you've selected for the front of your tree. Consider the pattern of the material. Take some time to position the template exactly where you want it, making sure you're honing in on a pretty section or focal point.

4 Flip the fabric over, pattern side down, and draw round your template directly onto the fabric with dressmaker's pen or pencil.

5 Whether you are using the same fabric or a different one for the back of your tree, place the two pieces together, pattern side facing pattern side (or if using plain fabric, front side facing front side) and secure with pins.

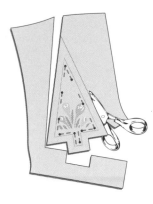

6 With a pair of sharp fabric scissors, cut around your tree shape leaving 1cm (⅜in) clear all round the guide line.

I made the error of snipping my tree shape a little too close to the guide line. Be sure to leave enough space clear to make stitching easier.

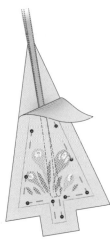

7 Cut a 20cm (8in) length of ribbon and fold flat into a loop shape. Slide the hanging loop upside down between the two fabric pieces and pin to secure until later.

Nimble fingers at the ready! Make absolutely sure that the top of your loop is lying flat inside your tree 'sleeve'. You're going to stitch the loop INTO the tree rather than stitching it onto the outside – this way, your loop is neat and super secure.

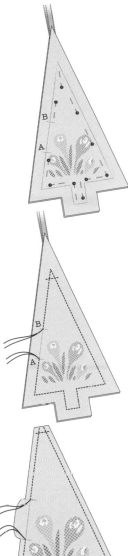

8 Designate a 'point A' on your guide line. Count 4cm (1½in) along from 'point A' and then mark 'point B' on your guide line.

9 Start stitching at point A and stop stitching at point B, leaving the 4cm (1½in) gap unstitched. You'll need this to turn your tree right side out and to pop the stuffing in.

10 With your scissors, cut round your sewn tree shape, removing the excess fabric and ribbon. Cut close to your stitch line, but be careful not to cut through it. Where you have left the gap, leave a little extra fabric to make it easier to stitch the gap shut once you have stuffed it.

Sharper Corners
When you finally turn your tree 'sleeve' right side out, you want your tree edges to be well defined and pointy. To reduce 'bunching' on the inside, make diagonal snips at the corners.

12 Fill your tree with wadding (batting). The stuffing from unwanted cushions or toys works just as well as new, store-bought craft wadding. If you're really stuck, you could even use cotton wool from your beauty cabinet.

Successful Stuffing
Don't try to cram big dollops of wadding straight into your tree sleeve. Instead, first form little radish-sized balls and stuff the edges and corners tight. Once the outer points of your tree feel fairly solid, start to fill the main 'body' of the tree with larger portions of wadding.

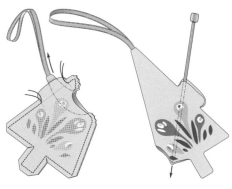

11 At the moment your fabric tree 'sleeve' is inside out. Now it's time to turn it round the right way. Use a knitting needle (or any long, thin, blunt object) to tease the tree sleeve and its pointy bits right side out.

Whatever your chosen poking device, undertake the task of pushing out the corners of your tree with care. Push too hard and you'll make a hole in your lovely stitching.

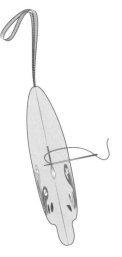

13 Now that your tree is stuffed, it's time to finish off your ornament. Push the extra fabric you left around the gap in your stitching back into the tree to leave a neat seam. Take your needle and thread and carefully sew it shut.

MEET THE MAKER: Kirsty Anderson

A keen collector of vintage fabrics and sewing ephemera, Kirsty's designs take old, found and thrifted items and transform them into whimsical interior adornments and off-beat wearables. Inherently organic in approach and theme, Kirsty's work takes inspiration from nature – foxes, birds, trees, clouds and mountains feature highly in her collections.

Tool of choice: Blunt knitting needle – ideal for stuffing soft interior decorations
Favourite designer: Fashion designer, Jessica Ogden
Inspired by: Taxidermy, the forest, vintage patterns and found objects
Most treasured possession: Glass pendant inherited from my grandmother
Favourite jam: Raspberry
Favourite crafting snack: Abernethy biscuits – rich, buttery sweet treats
Music to stitch by: Always!

STITCH IT UP A NOTCH

- So, you've made your first little hanging tree! Now, why not make a forest? These decorations make a marvellous visual impact when displayed on the wall in woodland-esque clusters. Experiment with colour, pattern and texture to create a calming yet fun and interesting textile feature.

- Fabric trims, lace strips, pretty ribbon, candy-striped twine or coarse packing string all make great hanging loops that will add a twist to the project. Incorporate treasures from your sewing stash. Embellish your trees with vintage buttons and pretty fixings – or embroider patterns or text as you wish. Make your tree your own!

- Add a handful of potpourri or dried herbs to your stuffing to transform your tree into a sweet-smelling pomander to hang in the kitchen, bathroom, cloakroom or wardrobe.

- By the time you've completed your forest task, you'll be stitching up little trees in your sleep. Move the project on and play with the shape and scale of your trees. I love the idea of making a set of oversized tree cushions – I can just imagine them nestling on my sofa!

Get Connected: Joining the Online Craft Community

Crafting makes for an ideal solo pursuit – a fun and productive way to wile away some rare quiet hours at home. Confining myself to my kitchen table with nothing for company but my craft kit, the radio and a bottle of rose lemonade is a treat I afford myself whenever time allows. However, there comes a point in every solitary crafter's life when you can't help but wonder if there are others like you. Who else is trying their hand at embroidering motifs onto napkins in preparation for a family meal? Who else has budding aspirations of building their own little craft empire? Once upon a time you may have struggled to find yourself a sociable nook in which to share your ideas and swap tips with other makers and hobbyists, but times they have a-changed. All over the world, busy crafters are linking up with each other and doing just that.

Don't panic – you needn't go too far from your comfy chair to build some relationships with likeminds. In fact, with your trusty laptop at the ready, you can jump right in and explore the ins and outs of the worldwide craft movement without even putting your tootsies in your shoesies.

Forums

Online craft forums have become popular gathering places for sharing information, tips and ideas. For every segment of the craft community, there's a forum for sociable web-savvy types to hang out and get to know one another. Some are practical in nature, designed for makers to swap 'how tos' and problem-solving tips. Some are more casual and serve as friendly spaces to chat and gossip about the latest crafty trends and community news. Finding and integrating yourself into a supportive craft forum can open up new opportunities and allow you to build friendships with other people who share your creative passions. Seek out a fun and lively forum attached to a craft group in your local area and you might even end up enjoying some real-life crafty collaborations!

On the flipside though, unbeknown to the suspecting rookie, community forums can be inherently tangled up in their own group politics and contributing to forum chatter when you're unfamiliar with the protocols, member hierarchies and offline relationships can unexpectedly land you in hot water. It's sometimes sensible to take up the role of the silent observer for a while before stomping in feet first. Who are the most active members? What are their affiliations? Has there been history of conflict over prickly topics in the past? What is reception like to 'newbies'? Once you feel more confident and you've established where you might fit in the forum, identify productive or interesting ways to contribute to current discussions, then pipe up and enjoy the fun!

Raising a Ruckus

What not to say in a craft forum …

- Hi folks. I'm new here. Would you like to buy my products?
- Eughk! Call that cross stitch? My two-year-old niece could do better.
- Please comment on my latest blog post. Please comment on my latest blog post.
- Please comment on my latest photograph. Please comment on my latest photograph.
- I saw this great handmade product online – does anyone know how I can copy it?

To attract regular visitors, I try to update the Made in the Shade blog several times a week.

The Made in the Shade Top 10 Crafty Blogs

I keep my eye on a select few wonderful blogs. To whet your appetite, you might want to bookmark these pages:

1. Indie Quarter
2. Print & Pattern
3. Poppytalk
4. Meet Me At Mike's
5. A Beautiful Mess
6. Make & Do With Perri
7. Design*Sponge
8. Fabric Nation
9. Craftzine
10. Holy Holy Guacamole

Blogs

Crafty Blog-o-rama Batman! Where to start? As someone who has been flirting with the blogosphere for several years (OK, so we're having an affair!), I have to admit that I still find the seemingly never-ending roll call of crafty and creative online blogs somewhat intimidating. As a partial technophobe, I do not possess the know-how (yet) to manage my blog reading effectively. I have several very competent friends and colleagues who organize their online lives meticulously and who somehow manage to unearth fantastic finds and interesting articles from indie craft sites on a daily basis. I look on in awe and thank them for forwarding me fabulous links now and again! I recommend befriending some of these web-trawling magpies.

A word of warning – it is very, very easy to become a blogoholic. You start virtually leafing through a beautiful blogsite, ooh-ing and aaah-ing at, I don't know – the loft workspace of a fancy designer – and before you know it, you've inadvertently been sucked into looking at 20 more sites and you've lost eight hours of your day. Catching up on some blog reading can provide a welcome distraction during an otherwise dull lunch break, but take it from someone who knows, it is wise to limit yourself! Even if you are justifying your blog browsing as 'research' – be sure that your research time doesn't seep into your planning and doing time.

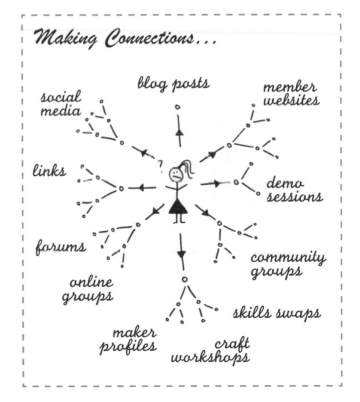

The Blogging Bug

So. You're no longer satisfied with just reading about other people's exploits in Craft Land, huh? Take a deep breath. Sit up straight! It's time to start a blog of your own. It is …

Just about everyone and, quite literally, their dog has a blog these days. Blogs serve different purposes for different people of course, but for the crafty girl, commonly the blog functions as a newsfeed, as a diary, a work log, a craft gallery, as a virtual learning and sharing space, and as a discussion forum. Publishing your own blog can be an exhilarating and empowering experience – regardless of whether you have a strong readership. Writing posts can feel a bit like talking to yourself aloud but you might also find that organizing your thoughts and ideas in a blog post is a really productive process. A sure fire way to make you do something is to blog about doing something. You have to follow up that gem of an idea if you've shared it with the world!

Share photos of you favourite tasty treats! Post recipes and invite reader reviews and comments. This snap of a Pin Up Girl cocktail was taken during a trip away and featured on the Made in the Shade summer holiday blog post.

As a new blogger, you might find the process of writing your own posts a bit scary at first. Try not to worry about whether you are typing too much or too little. Over time and with practice, you will settle into your own writing and editing groove. If writing really isn't your forte, this doesn't mean you can't run a successful and popular blog. Your posts might become more image led and your writing more like accompanying captions. Indeed, sites like Tumblr cater specifically for this style of online posting. If the opposite is true and you find yourself writing and writing and writing, then you might need to work a little harder to make sure your posts are gripping enough to capture your

I Blog Therefore I Am

The key to writing an engaging craft blog is to team 'show and tell' gallery and news elements with some more personal touches. It is interesting to (virtually) thumb through pages of someone's craft catalogue, but after a while it can become a bit tedious. People are inherently curious (read 'nosey') creatures. Not only do they want to see what you've been making lately but they also want to know why you made it, where you made it, and even what you were eating while you were making it! They'll also want to know where you found the beautiful vase in the background of your last project pic! Inject a dose of personality into your posts and you'll have 'em hooked.

I've come across some lovely 'personal touch' blog elements. I particularly enjoy features like What I Wore Today (have a look at the Flickr group) or blogs with over-arching themes like A Dress A Day. I also love to snoop around designer-makers' workspaces and it's great to meet their friends – and even their pets! Since this section is encouraging you to inject a bit of yourself into your blog, it might seem a bit odd for me to offer too much advice (for I am not you), but if you are really stuck for inspiration, you could always try out some of these ideas …

- Share your personal culinary tastes and post a recipe for your very favourite dish – encourage your readers to try it out. They could even send you pictures or reviews afterwards?

- Gather together a collection of belongings and artefacts from your house, room by room and photograph them. Showcase your most treasured possessions in themed galleries.

- The next time you return from a shopping trip with a sackful of goodies, why not share your haul with your readers? One of my favourite pastimes is to drool at other people's thrifty finds online.

- Over time, readers from all over the world will start to pass through your blog pages. Show visitors what your neighbourhood is like. Write a post about local landmarks or make a little film, giving readers a virtual tour of your city/town.

reader. Scrolling through your blog page should be fun and inspiring for your online guests – not too laborious. Whenever you tap out an epic post, give it a quick edit before you click 'publish' just to double-check that the content is interesting and to the point. Provide links to the people, places and things you talk about. Paste beautiful images to illustrate your post and offer directions to other topically relevant websites and blogs where you can.

Stitching Together a Virtual Social Network

You most likely have your own social networking profiles already. A Facebook page maybe? Or a Twitter account? If you're anything like me, you probably spend an inordinate amount of time tinkering around with social media, but – are you using your online links to their full crafty potential? You needn't use your online life exclusively to satisfy crafty ends, but I bet your friends and colleagues would enjoy the odd peep at your handmade creations now and again. Using your Facebook profile and Twitter feed to direct people to your blog posts is also a super-productive way to attract new readers. Understanding crafting comrades will offer consolation in times of crafting calamity and they'll congratulate you on your creative successes. Most of your favourite designer-makers and indie shops and galleries will have an online presence on free public sites like these too – link up with them. Make contact, show your support or just keep up to date with everything they're up to.

Add variety and the all-important personal touch to your blog by giving readers a peek into your home life. This snap of me and my husband was taken in our living room on 14 February and featured on our Valentine blog post.

Stitching Together a Real–Life Social Network

Meeting friends and creative contacts online is fun and can be very fruitful, but it's just not the same as getting together in real-life, is it? You might not know it yet, but I can guarantee that nearby, there is a craft group or stitchin' meet-up just waiting to happen – if it's not happening already, of course! The stitch 'n' bitch session is a staple now in lots of bars and cafes, and crafty workshops, skills swaps, casual demo sessions and craft-a-longs are becoming increasing popular. Heck! I guess my town is particularly lucky in that it boasts a cake shop for knitters, a sewing cafe, a few exciting workshop spaces, a couple of great supplies stores and a healthy catalogue of crafty groups and meet-ups. If, in your vicinity, you're a little bit less spoilt for choice for ways to get involved in the real-life craft community, fret not. You always have the option to start up your own little network and grow your own community from scratch. There are members just waiting to join. I know it.

Make real-life craft connections by organizing your own meet-up in a local venue – and don't forget to blog about it afterwards!

PHONE HOME

by Susie Maroon

The busy girl's mobile phone is the buzzy hub around which her life is organized: arrangements are made, reminders are set, emails are answered, Twitter updates are posted and emergency craft supplies are ordered. Thank your phone for keeping you connected by making it its very own home. Complete with a durable leather outer and protective felt inner, this pouch will keep your phone safe and scratch-free. It looks rather swish too!

Project Notes

Susie Maroon is one of my favourite designer makers. I was delighted to be invited into her little nest of creative activity. Despite my questionable drawing skills and my seemingly weak arm muscles, I was pleased as punch to leave the crafting session with my very own handmade Phone Home. Do you want to hear a secret? I was allowed to make two versions of the project. I stitched one by hand and then Susie afforded me the honour of trying out a second design using her fancy embroidery machine. 'Tis quite a fabulous contraption!

Susan Brown, the designer and tutor in this project, runs her own design label, Susie Maroon. Flick to the end of the project for a peep into her creative world. Throughout our stitching session, I was seriously drooling at her wonderfully organized, super-stylish home-studio. What I would give for a craft nook like that …

Pleased as punch… ☑
Crafting calamity… ☐

Get ready to show off… ✿ your basic drawing skills ✿ your hand stitching skills ✿ your machine sewing skills

SEWING BOX ESSENTIALS

- ❀ 1–2mm (⅛in) bookbinder's leather, 50cm (20in) square
- ❀ Craft felt, 50cm (20in) square
- ❀ Tear-away stabilizer (such as Stitch & Tear), 30cm (12in) square
- ❀ Small hand embroidery hoop (padded with muslin to protect the leather)
- ❀ Sharp large-eye needle
- ❀ Embroidery threads
- ❀ Leather sewing-machine needle
- ❀ Metal ruler
- ❀ Tweezers
- ❀ Stitching awl (optional)
- ❀ Basic tool kit (see Getting Started)

1 Measure your phone – then add 5mm (⅛in) to both the length and width measurements to arrive at the dimensions you will need.

2 Cut your leather, felt and tear-away stabilizer into 20cm (8in) squares. Cut two of leather, two of felt and one of tear-away stabilizer. You might find it easier to cut your leather using a leather or craft knife and cutting mat.

3 With a pencil, sketch a rectangle (according to the dimensions calculated in step 1) onto the tear-away stabilizer. Add a simple line drawing of your desired motif into the rectangle, positioned just where you want it.

Another Option
If you don't want to use tear-away stabilizer or you don't have any to hand, you can draw your motif lightly onto the leather itself using the point of a stitch picker.

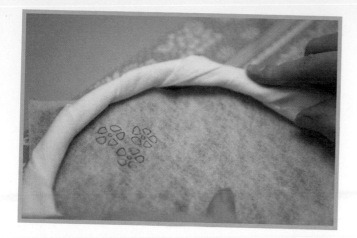

Guide Grid

If you happen to have a stitching awl to hand (and let's face it, who doesn't?!), you can make the sewing process a little easier on yourself. Punch holes at regular intervals along your line drawing and use them as a DIY stitching grid.

6 Once you have finished stitching your design, un-hoop your fabric and layer the stitched pieces together with the remaining pieces of felt and leather so that the leather is on the outside.

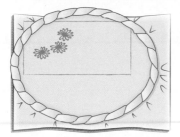

4 Layer one piece of felt on the bottom, one piece of leather in the middle and the tear-away stabilizer with your drawing on it on the top and secure the fabrics into your padded embroidery hoop.

5 Using a sharp large-eye needle and coloured embroidery thread, stitch over the outline of your drawing using a decorative running stitch, chain stitch or cross stitch. Alternatively, stitch over your drawing outline using your desired decorative stitch on your sewing machine fitted with a leather needle.

Embroidery threads are usually six strands thick but you can separate them to your desired thickness if you are doing hand embroidery on this project.

Remember, Remember When Working With Leather ...

- Don't be scared! Leather is much more workable and durable than you might think.

- Consider your stitching strategy carefully. Once you puncture the leather, the hole is there for good so don't rush. Take your time and make sure you are happy with your design and the stitch you are using. If you have some spare scraps to hand, practice first.

- Be kind to your leather. Try not to scrape it, scratch it or stretch it. Handle it with care.

- If you decide that you like this sewing on leather lark and you want to experiment more, then get to it! Be careful when choosing motifs though. Try to steer clear of designs with very close stitches and lots of filled areas. You run the risk of cutting the shape of the design into the leather. You don't want to perforate a big hole in your project. No, no.

Be Kind to Your Leather

While thin, supple leather is easier to sew onto than thick, rigid leather, it is notoriously difficult to manage in that it is easily marked or stretched out of shape. Take extra care of your leather during the hooping and sewing process by placing muslin sheets around the edge of your top hoop. This will help create a soft protective layer for your leather. Do not leave your fabrics in the hoop any longer than necessary. Removing them quickly will prevent the indent of the hoop transferring onto your leather and leaving an unsightly mark.

To get satin stitch, just reduce the spacing on your zigzag stitch function.

8 Place your pouch onto the cutting mat and with a leather knife or craft scalpel, trim the pouch along the edge of a metal ruler leaving 2mm (⅛in) at the bottom and on each side and 1cm (⅜in) at the top. Make sure not to cut through the stitches holding the pouch together.

9 Finally, tear away the stabilizer to reveal your stitching on the leather. Use a pair of tweezers to remove any small pieces around the intricate parts of your embroidery.

7 Using the satin stitch function on your sewing machine and with the leather needle still fitted, sew the pouch along three edges of the rectangle you have drawn onto the tear-away stabilizer leaving an opening at the top.

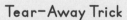

Tear-Away Trick
Remove the tear-away stabilizer in a sideways motion. This will allow you to pull it clean away without disturbing your stitches.

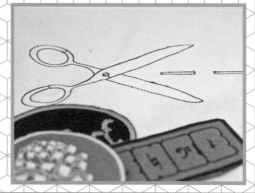

MEET THE MAKER: Susan Brown

Textile designer and artist Susan Brown is the ever-smiley faced maven of style behind eco-label, Susie Maroon. Taking sparks of inspiration from processes, lists, instruction manuals and doodles, Susie's homeware and accessories collections feature beautifully embroidered motifs teamed with luscious, understated colourways. Susie works with leather – a lot – stitching up cushions, belts and bunting to name a few of her creations. She rescues skins from a local tannery that would otherwise be sent to landfill. Pretty neat, huh?

Tool of choice: My new concealed zipper foot – I used to hate zips, now I love them

Inspired by: Mighty talented people, the low light in winter, humour, music, old things, new things, things…

Favourite designers/artists: Claire Barclay, Richard Saja, Janet Cardiff and George Bures Miller, FOUND Electronics, Julia Douglas

Most treasured possession: The tiny wooden chair I used as a little girl – was my bottom really that small?

Interesting fact: I like to undertake guerilla DIY projects – so keep your house keys in your pockets!

STITCH IT UP A NOTCH

- Adorning your Phone Home with a simple embroidered or machine-stitched motif makes for a sleek and stylish end result. However, if you're partial to crafty embellishments, introduce buttons, appliqué shapes, charms and sparkle as you see fit. Go wild!

- If you have a leather punch handy, you might want to round off the edges of your phone pouch with a chic curved effect.

- Transform the pouch from phone cover to spectacle case by elongating it. Punch holes in the top opening of the case and thread beautiful ribbon through to make a simple but pretty closure.

- Another of the busy girl's indispensable gizmos is her laptop. A window to the online craft community and a trusty blogging sidekick, the busy girl's computer holds all her important files and crafty archives. Supersize the pouch to fit and whip up your own luxurious leather laptop sleeve too.

APPLES & PEARS APRON

by Miso Funky

Add a little touch of crafty glamour to your favourite apron or liven up a boring old kitchen cover-up with these cute, culinary cross stitch motifs. Fruity! The Apples & Pears Apron is a simple project but requires time, patience and stitching stamina.

Project Notes

I was really excited about this project. I'd always had a hankering to try my hand at cross stitch. With Claire's tuition (and encouragement), my little pear turned out just as I hoped it would. On leaving Claire's workroom, I was gifted a little cross stitch kit of my own to take home. My next crafty task? To stitch myself some cherries to adorn my favourite frock!

Claire Brown of Miso Funky is best known for her stitching prowess and as such is the perfect guide to show me the basics of cross stitch. Read about Claire's penchant for 80s TV shows and find out what her most treasured possessions are in the Meet the Maker section at the end of the project.

Pleased as punch... ☑

Crafting calamity... ☐

Get ready to show off... ❀ your basic hand stitching skills ❀ your chart reading skills

SEWING BOX ESSENTIALS

- ✿ Apron
- ✿ Waste canvas
- ✿ Embroidery needle
- ✿ Embroidery threads in green, red and brown
- ✿ Tweezers
- ✿ Basic tool kit (see Getting Started)

Before we start, you need to pick your perfect pinny. Let's thrift and reuse! I love vintage aprons – the one I chose was a gift from Made in the Shade gal, Clare. It's a pale pink gingham fabric and the perfect shade to match my motifs.

Waste Not, Want Not

Waste canvas – not the prettiest of names, really. However, contrary to its unfortunate title, waste canvas is a super-useful little fella to have in your sewing kit. This gridded fabric acts as a guide for cross stitches. The grid helps get the needle through the right holes, in the right position, aiding a gap-free, even finish to the design. Waste canvas allows you to cross stitch onto any fabric, not just evenweave materials. Neat!

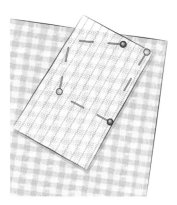

1 Choose which design to start with – apple or pear – and decide where you want to position it on your apron. Cut a piece of waste canvas large enough to leave 4–5cm (1½–2in) clear all round the design, then pin the waste canvas onto the chosen section of the apron.

As a busy girl, you might not have the time nor the inclination to spend time meticulously pinning your waste fabric onto your pinny in a perfectly straight line – so why not position your motif on a slightly jaunty horizontal? Go on, just whang it on!

2 Cut a length of embroidery thread roughly 30cm (12in) long and separate it into lots of two strands. The colour of thread you need will be dictated by which fruit you are stitching – follow the chart (see Templates). Thread your needle and tie a knot at the end.

4 Form the first leg of the first cross and then complete the row of half crosses, missing out any stitches that are in a different colour.

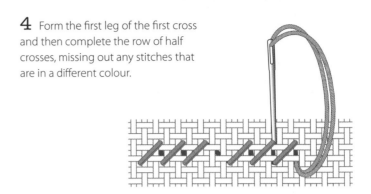

Gridlock
The cross stitch chart (or pattern) is a grid that shows you where to put your stitches and which colours of thread to use. In the case of our pear motif, we're using just two colours – brown and green. A green stitch is indicated on the chart (see Templates) by a green square and a brown stitch is indicated by a brown square. What could be more simple?

5 When you reach the end of the row, stitch back along, completing the second leg of each cross.

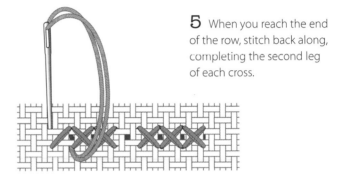

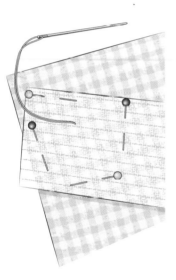

3 To start stitching, follow the fruit pattern from the bottom row up. Take your threaded needle to the underside of the apron and locate the centre of the square you are starting with. Draw the thread through the hole slowly, taking care to keep it running smoothly.

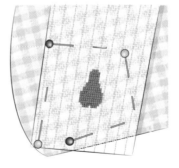

6 Follow the pattern, cross stitching until you have completed all the stitches in the first colour.

I got a little over excited with my stitching and managed to get tangled up a few times! Take your time …

7 To finish off your thread, weave the end in and out of the back of your stitches a few times to secure then snip off any excess thread.

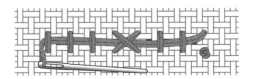

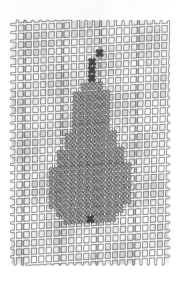

8 Take two strands of the other colour, thread the needle and knot as before. Follow the chart to finish the motif and weave in the ends of the thread as before.

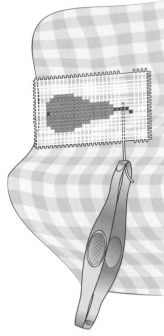

10 Using tweezers, draw out individual waste canvas threads. Hold your stitching in place to prevent it from being pulled or distorted. Tug the tweezers firmly – but slowly and carefully.

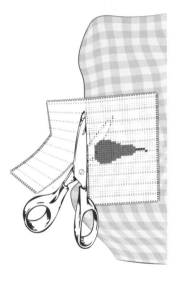

9 Once your cute cross stitch fruit shape is complete, you will need to remove the waste canvas from the apron. Trim the excess canvas from around the design, leaving 1cm (⅜in) clear all the way round. Fray the edges with your fingers as you go.

11 When you have removed all the waste canvas threads, you are left with the finished motif on your apron. Now, start all over again and get going on that second fruit pattern!

Caution! Be careful not to cut through your pinny when trimming away the excess waste canvas.

Removing Threads
When you're drawing out your waste canvas threads, it's much more productive to tease out all the vertical threads first and then all the horizontal threads rather than trying to do a bit of both.

MEET THE MAKER: Claire Brown

Subversive cross stitcher Claire Brown designs and makes witty and humorous interiors pieces and alternative gifts under the Miso Funky moniker. She adorns everything from cushions and tea towels to coasters and fridge magnets with her cheeky slogans. Miso Funky samplers are snapped up by customers all over the world. Rumour has it even British domestic goddess Delia Smith owns one!

Tool of choice: A needle and thread

Interesting fact: I can count to ten in seven languages

Inspired by: Historical cross stitch, found objects and overheard conversations

Favourite designer-maker: Heidi Kenney aka My Paper Crane

Favourite food: My husband's curry

Most treasured possession: A little box of junk my granny left me when she died. I used to play with it when I was little – she would gather odds and sods and pop them into the box – growing my collection of treasure all the time

Crafting companion: 80s British sit-com, *Hi-De-Hi*

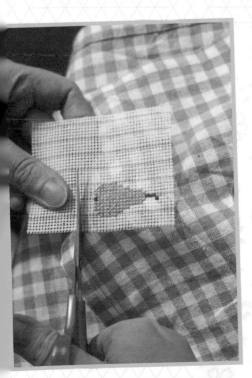

STITCH IT UP A NOTCH

- Use these patterns to sew yourself up a whole range of complementary table linen and kitchenware. Cross stitch your apples and pears onto napkins, tablecloths, worktop protectors, fridge magnets and tea towels.

- Why not try sketching out your own cross stitch patterns? Invest in a squared paper pad and experiment with shapes and colours. Create other fruit designs – cherries or strawberries might be fun? Or come up with something entirely different!

- Why not try your hand at stitching text? You could go on to add a fruity slogan, (I like 'Hey good lookin'! Whatcha got cookin'?') in between your cute fruit motifs and make a framed sampler to hang proudly on your kitchen wall.

- You might want to take your new-found love of simple cross stitch out of the kitchen all together. Wear your pear with pride and try embellishing the pocket of your favourite shirt or the corner of your tote bag, coin purse or spectacle case.

ANYTHING GOES MEMORY ART

by Jolene Crawford

To the busy crafter, the mere mention of quilting might seem intimidating, fiddly and time consuming – a highly involved project that only seasoned pros ought to embark upon. Stop right there. Not so. In this 'anything goes' project, we leave behind stuffy notions of quilting and we ditch the quilting rule book. Have some fun piecing together a fabric made entirely from personal swatches in manageable chunks to make a statement piece of textile art.

Project Notes

Until my making session with Jolene, I'd never really felt drawn to quilting as a craft endeavour. However, Jolene's approach is refreshing, accessible and the end result is beautiful and unusual. Offering a contemporary twist on an age-old tradition, this project has me hooked and my mind is now set on stitching up a memoir. I am pleased as punch with my 'anything goes' art. This little square marks the first of many and the start of an ongoing personal project.

Keen crafter Jolene Crawford kindly agreed to demo one of her favourite quilting projects for me – teaching me step by step how to make my own version. Learn about Jolene, her influences, passions and favourite crafty blogs at the end of the project.

Pleased as punch... ☑

Crafting calamity... ☐

Get ready to show off...
✿ your imagination   ✿ your confidence   ✿ those nimble fingers
✿ your basic machine stitching skills   ✿ your basic measuring and cutting skills

SEWING BOX ESSENTIALS

- ✿ Variety of fabric scraps and remnants
- ✿ Rotary cutter
- ✿ Perspex ruler/omnigrid
- ✿ Frame or mount of your choice
- ✿ Basic tool kit (see Getting Started)

1 First, mark and cut a square measuring roughly 5 x 5cm (2 x 2in). This will go on to be the central square of the project, the core piece around which all other stitching will be based.

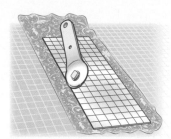

2 Using a rotary cutter and cutting mat, trim a variety of fabrics into strips measuring roughly 3 x 30cm (1 x 12in). Start off with about 30 strips. Keep some fabric pieces handy should you need to top up your stock of strips later.

Clever Cutting

You can, of course, use scissors for cutting but I guarantee once you complete your first quilted square for your memory art, you will want to make more. In the long term, the rotary cutter is much handier for this type of work.

3 Take around a third of your 30cm (12in) strips and slice them in half.

These 15cm (6in) strips will be useful. We will start the patchwork with small strips initially and they get longer and longer as the stitching progresses. Having some shorter strips to hand saves time and minimizes wastage.

4 Take your central square and one of your short fabric strips. Place the strip along the top side of your central square, pattern side to pattern side. Position your strip at a chirpy, jaunty angle cutting across one corner.

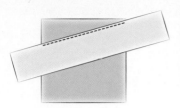

5 Using your sewing machine set to a straight stitch, sew the strip onto the central square a few millimetres in from the edge of the strip then trim the excess threads close to the fabric.

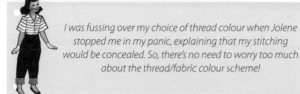

I was fussing over my choice of thread colour when Jolene stopped me in my panic, explaining that my stitching would be concealed. So, there's no need to worry too much about the thread/fabric colour scheme!

Safe Stitching

Usually you would double back on your stitching (or use your machine's Lock Off function, if it has one) at the start and at the end of your sewing line to secure the stitches, but there's no real need to do that here. Your stitches will become more and more secure as we carry on making our square. Don't fret over loose ends – all will be well!

6 Using your rotary cutter and cutting mat, and with the aid of a Perspex ruler, trim off the excess central square fabric beyond the top of your sewn-on strip.

7 Ensuring your iron is set to the appropriate temperature for the fabrics you are working with, iron the strip in place, pattern side up.

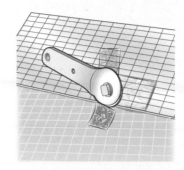

8 Return to the cutting mat and using your rotary cutter and Perspex ruler, trim off the excess fabric at either end of your strip to make flush lines all round your shape.

9 Working round your central square in a clockwise direction, repeat steps 4–8 until you have sewn one strip round each side of your central square.

After a few repeats I felt comfortable enough to have a little bit of fun with my jaunty angles and the positioning of my strips. The instructions might sound complicated, but when you get going, you'll be able to carry on without even referring to them!

Anything Goes!

From this point on, you will notice that there is always one side of your shape with three different fabric swatches on show. The other sides will just have two. The side with three fabric swatches is now always the side you lay your next strip onto. It's also helpful to use the left side peak of the shape as the corner you make your jaunty angle with. To keep a spontaneous, free-and-easy feel to the project, vary the gradient of the angle to suit. Sometimes uniformly working to the left peak all the time creates an overly pointy shape, so, whenever you feel like it, add a strip through the right corner just to even things up a little bit.

The great thing about this project is, even if you make a mistake, it doesn't really matter. If you feel you need to unpick, then unpick, but you can always just persevere, knowing that in the end, your hiccups will be disguised and eventually add to the charm and spontaneous feel of your memory art.

11 As before, cut the excess from beyond the top of the strip, iron the strip flat pattern side up and cut the excess from the ends of the strip where necessary.

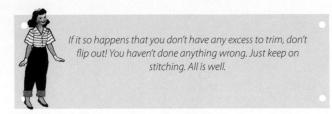

If it so happens that you don't have any excess to trim, don't flip out! You haven't done anything wrong. Just keep on stitching. All is well.

12 Continue to work round your shape over and over again until you have the perfect size to fit in your chosen frame/mount. As the patchwork piece grows you will need to use the longer strips. You may need to cut more strips, depending on the size of the finished piece you want. When you are satisfied that your shape is complete, give it a final iron, check it over for loose threads and trim any straggly bits.

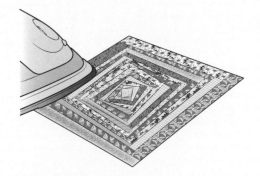

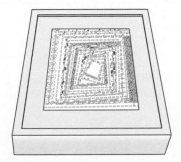

10 With the three-fabric-swatch side at the top of your shape, lay a strip of fabric in place, over the left corner at an angle. Then stitch the strip, pattern side to pattern side, onto your shape using a plain stitch on your sewing machine.

13 All that's left to do now is to mount your memory art in your frame and hang or prop it proudly!

MEET THE MAKER: Jolene Crawford

With a professional background in media, television and the arts, Jolene Crawford is a mother, musician and indie business owner, working hard to promote and contribute to the creative fabric of her local community. A keen collector and charity-shop scourer, Jolene is driven to make and craft by her desire to give treasurable gifts to friends and family and to avoid buying soulless mass-produced items from chain stores.

Tool of choice: My sewing machine – a gift from my mother

Inspired by: My mother, my grandmother, nostalgia, people-watching and the city I live in

Favourite blogs: A Beautiful Mess, Something's Hiding In Here and The Selby

Favourite creative people: Interior designer, Abigail Ahern, folk artist Julie Arkell and stylist, author and boutique owner, Emily Chalmers

Most treasured possession: My mum's handmade Shetland jumpers from the 1970s and my collection of vintage mirrors

Crafting soundtrack: BBC Radio 4 and the World Service

Favourite crafty tipple: An endless supply of tea – maybe with a slice of home-baked banana cake

Interesting fact: My mother and I have matching tattoos

STITCH IT UP A NOTCH

- Build up your collection of memory art squares over time to make your own memory quilt. Make a quilt as a gift for a loved one or stitch up your own life story.

- Experiment using different widths of fabric strips to create an unusual, higgledy-piggledy finish with lots of movement and texture.

- Sew up a supersized square and incorporate it as the front of a handmade cushion.

- Using fabric contributions gathered from friends and loved ones, stitch up a prize present for a special occasion – a significant birthday or anniversary, a new baby or just for fun! Present your memory gift accompanied by a handmade card. Paste tiny swatches of the fabrics you've been given by other people into the card, listing who donated which fabric. What a lovely idea!

Let's Have a Party: Hosting Crafty Get-Togethers

With home-supper clubs, living-room gigs and clothes-swap parties dubbed 'the new going out', why not get in touch with your inner homebird? Rather than trotting along in the rain to the local stitch 'n' bitch, round up some friends and host your very own stitching session in the comfort of your own lounge. Or – go one better and host a crafty party, the likes of which will be the talk of the your local craft circle for months! You in? Oh, I do love a good party …

Venue

OK. So. The party is in your house. This much we know. However, you might want to play hostess in just one designated room – or you might want to open your whole living space. Of course, the scope and scale of your party will be determined by the size of your home and the number of crafty guests you can drum up. If you are lucky enough to have a dining kitchen with a big table to sit round, then this might make for a perfect setting. Or a cosy living room with some sit-down floor space would lend itself well too. If you decide to go all out, you could theme activities in fitting with every room in your house!

Theme

Ordinarily, the mere mention of a 'themed' party sends shivers down my spine. And not in a good way. I worry that I need to wear a silly costume or partake in a dreaded role-play game. However, there are ways to theme a crafty party without striking fear into your guests!

Why not develop a theme around materials – wool, fabric, wood or paper? I have a long-time obsession with paper. When I was a little girl and my sisters would ask me what I'd like as a birthday or Christmas gift, I'd simply answer, 'paper'. Still now, my friends and relations know that I will always be thrilled to be gifted a notebook or ream of coloured paper, a writing set or some vintage airmail envelopes. In taking paper as an example party theme (I am simply giddy at the thought), then we can feature it in every aspect of your party, from the invitations and the decorations, to the snacks and drinks and even the music and activities.

Decor

The busy party hostess may be tempted to bypass the more fiddly, finer details of her get-together and do away with decorations. Just imagine though, how impressed your guests would be to find that you had 'thrown together' some beautiful paper flower garlands or a few strings of hand-cut bunting especially for the occasion. These projects needn't take up too much of your precious time and in terms of cost, they are virtually free. Think creatively. Go wild! Come up with your own ideas too.

Easy-Peasy DIY 'Flower' Garland

Gather together a pile of unwanted paper samples – you can use everything from large envelopes, newspapers, pages from books and conventional (but interesting) sheets. Your paper pieces don't need to be uniform in size, but the largest should probably be no bigger than 8cm (3in) square. Making mismatched 'flowers' will add to the charm of your handmade decoration.

Make your paper pieces into little cone shapes. Curl the paper round itself, making a point at one end and an open base at the other. Secure with a little bit of clear tape. Lay out a length of string (as long as you want your garland to be) and attach the point ends of your DIY 'flower' with a little more tape. Done! Hang your garlands over pictures, off door handles or round window frames.

Super-Quick Bunting

Again, gather together unwanted paper samples. Cut them freehand into triangle shapes. With a craft knife, cut out shapes and patterns, or perhaps letters to spell out a party message. Fold the base of each triangle in a centimetre or two. Cut a length of string (as long as you want your string of bunting to be). Slide the string into the fold on the triangle shape and secure with tape. Et voila! Drape bunting round your front door or over your mantle.

Guest List and Invitations

Are you throwing a party to convert your not-so-creative chums to the church of craft? Or are you more keen to get together with gals and guys that already have a penchant for the DIY approach and might be able to swap skills or supplies? You decide! Both options open up loads of opportunities for fun – but beware that you might end up playing hostess less and tutor more if you plump purely for craft-virgin guests. Why not mix it up – invite both groups but assign your novice pals a stitching buddy – allowing you to stitch with one hand and pour the gin with the other? (Oh my! This could be the beginning of a beautiful friendship. Craft dating!)

To follow in the home-supper club/living-room gig trend, you might fancy broadening out your party to friends of friends or third-link friends. In theory I do love this idea, but in practice, I'm personally not quite adventurous or carefree enough for all that. It's up to you though. Go for it. But stay safe.

With paper as the theme, your invitations can embody the feel and style of your gathering. Handwrite hardcopy invitations on scraps of beautiful papers from your collection. A mixture of plain, coloured, brown, lined, squared or graph will make for a fitting opener to your crafty knees-up. It might be fun to send your invitations in the style of a ransom note? Cut out individual letters and characters from newspapers and magazines (picking the prettiest fonts of course) and paste them onto your invitation. Or – if you can hold your own in the Photoshop area, why not design your own invitation incorporating lots of different vintage wallpaper designs? Layer up, baby!

Refreshments and Snacks

Well now. Your paper theme is easy to incorporate here! If you've decided that making flower garlands was quite enough effort, then why not take a time-efficient route to refreshments by simply dishing up oh-so-easy ovenable snacks and tasty drinkables … on paper plates, paper doillies, paper cups and paper napkins? To add a last-minute crafty touch, you could always punch pretty designs into your napkins and plates! (You thought I was exaggerating about the paper obsession thing didn't you? I really wasn't).

If you are in full party-planning swing though and you want to knock your guests' socks off with your attention to detail, then you might like these ideas:

- Whip up a batch of cupcakes and top them with paper embellishments. You can buy edible paper – and even edible ink to add a personalized touch to your cakes.
- Wrap individual bite-sized versions of your favourite sweeties – maybe coconut ice or peppermint slice – in a layer of greaseproof paper then wrap again in brown and graph paper. Pop a little sticker on to secure or tie with paper ribbon. These will look fabulous stacked up on … why, your paper serving plate of course.
- Send your friends back to their childhood days. Hunt down some packs of wafer paper for everyone to nibble on.

Music

Music is integral to creating any party atmosphere. You must, must, must think about your soundtrack. One of my favourite aspects of arranging a get-together at home is deciding on the music. Make a digital playlist for computer or iPod playback – or pre-make CD compilations ahead of the event. If you're feeling flush and have enough time, you could always make your guests a little party favour of a selection of themed songs. Naturally, the CD will be wrapped in a paper pocket!

The Made in the Shade Top 5 Party Songs

In keeping the spirit of things, you might want to seek out these hits:

1. 'Paper Roses' – Loretta Lynn
2. 'Paperback Writer' – The Beatles
3. 'Paper Doll' – The Mills Brothers
4. 'Pretty Paper' – Roy Orbison
5. 'It's Only a Paper Moon' – Ella Fitzgerald

Or – anything and everything by Pulp!

Activities

Now, I know the prospect of a paper party is incredibly exciting, but don't forget the main reason you are gathering your guests together. You are hosting a crafty party. So what sort of creative activities might you provide? This could be your perfect chance to demo that new project you've mastered, encouraging all your friends to craft-a-long. Or maybe you want to stage some speed-crafting activity? Lay out a selection of supplies, set the timer, and watch your guests craft up a storm under pressure! To see the paper theme appear in your craft itinerary, perhaps you ask your guests to bring some artefacts that can be made into a take-away collage by the end of the night – or get everyone together to try their hand at some simple paper cutting. If you would rather your party was a bit more freeform, you could always follow the stitch 'n' bitch format and invite everyone to bring their current sewing project, enjoy some party treats, chat, enjoy each other's company and learn a tip or two.

Once you've seen your first house party go off with a giggle, you will want to repeat your success as social butterfly. Maybe next time you might want to try out these ideas:

- For a thrifty way to bag some new craft supplies, fabrics and patterns, make your next get-together a supplies swap. Encourage your guests to bring five usable craft supplies they would like to offload and let the swapping, bartering and elbow jabbing begin!

- My friend Eva threw a party once where everyone invited was required to make a bag and fill it with surprise gifts. On arrival at the party, everyone was given a raffle ticket. Each bag was displayed on a table at one end of the room and assigned a different raffle ticket number to that of the bag maker. During the party, tickets were drawn. Every guest who brought a bag left with a new bag – handmade by another guest. Try this – it is so much fun.

- Turn your living room into a giant trunk sale. Make a few extra bucks from your excess trinkets and one-time treasures by filling your front room with all the homewares, craft supplies, books, magazines, textiles and clothes you no longer need. Put a price label on absolutely everything and let your guests eye up potential bargains while you socialize over a bowl of party punch.

After a few rip-roaring get-togethers you might find that you're a bit of a whizz at this party planning malarkey. You might also find that you've embraced the 'stay at home' trend quite enough. Seek out opportunities in local venues, bars, cafes and community halls – you could easily bring your party pizzazz to a wider audience by taking your ideas out of your living room and into the community. Maybe it's time to offer fellow craft enthusiasts a fresh alternative to the old stitch 'n' bitch. Get on it!

FOUR HOURS OR LESS

The cosy comfort items and stylish wearables featured in this section are a little more complicated and time consuming than those we found in chapter 2, however, chunk 'em up and you will stitch through them in no time. This little icon  indicates an ideal stopping point in the project – a point where you can easily pick up where you left off in your next session. Hoorah for chunking! Feature articles focus on using your sewing to spruce up your local community and make strangers smile, as well as providing some hints and tips for developing your hobby and taking your work out into the world of the craft fair.

3

CRAFTY FOX CUSHION

by Michelle Aaron

Made entirely from reclaimed fabric and scraps of felt, this cushion is a freeform, 'fly by the seat of your pants' sewing project that encourages you to cut loose and have some fun. This cheeky fella is the perfect couch companion – spend some quality time with your bushy tailed pillow while stitching or reading up on some project inspirations.

Project Notes

Not one to adhere to rules and pernickety patterns, Michelle encouraged me to play with her project and make it my own. I was not at all convinced that my limited machine sewing skills would see me through – I envisioned my Crafty Fox emerging from the sewing machine holey and misshapen. Now, don't let me fool you, this task was not all plain sailing. There were a few worrying moments, but we laughed our way through and in the end all was well. Yes, my fox is a little smaller than I'd anticipated. Yes, his face is enormous. Yes, he has slightly deformed ears and a weirdly non-bushy tail. But I love him!

Exercising the patience of a saint, compulsive crafter Michelle Aaron led me through the Crafty Fox project step by step (with a little refuel break for a bowl of home-made ice cream!). Meet her at the end of the project.

Pleased as punch... ☑

Crafting calamity... ☐

Get ready to show off... ✿ your imagination ✿ your basic drawing and cutting skills
✿ your machine sewing skills ✿ your basic hand sewing skills

1 Fold your fabric in half, wrong sides together. With dressmaker's pen, draw the outline of your fox shape. Draw round the shape again, leaving 3cm (1in) clearance. Using the outer line as a guide, cut out the shape. With the fabric folded you will cut two identical shapes – one will become the fox's front and one will become the back.

2 To make your fox face, cut a kidney-bean shaped oval from a sheet of orange felt to fit onto the head portion of the fox body. Again, you can sketch the shape first if you like or you can cut freestyle.

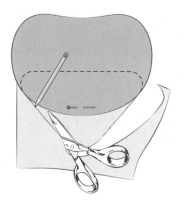

3 For foxy's chin, pin the bottom edge of the orange felt face over the top edge of your white felt. Sketch a rounded triangle shape onto the white felt, lining up the width and depth in proportion to the fox face and cut out.

Try a Template

Drawing is definitely not my forte. I was really nervous about creating my fox shape on the fabric. Michelle made a mini template in advance of our lesson. I placed it next to me and used it as a guide. I looked at the template and guided my pen to make a supersized version. You might want to give this a try. Or if you prefer to, sketch up a freeform fox. Knock yourself out!

4 Fold the remainder of the white felt in half. With the fabric doubled, cut out an oval to make two identical eye shapes. Use the orange felt face as a guide to proportions.

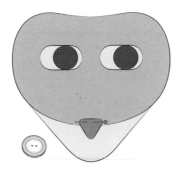

5 Using a small circular object (such as a coin or a button) as a template, cut out two circles from a scrap of black felt. Then cut out a rounded triangle from a scrap of brown felt to make a little nose and position in the centre of the face. Put a pin through all the layers to hold them in place.

Chunk!

6 With black thread, hand sew the black circles onto the whites of the eyes. The position of the pupils will determine his personality. Before you sew them, position both the eye layers (white and black) onto the orange face and experiment with different expressions.

7 With brown thread, hand sew the felt nose shape into position – between the orange face and white chin. Then, using white thread, hand sew the eyes onto the face.

8 Using your sewing machine and orange thread, stitch the white felt chin shape to the orange felt face, leaving just the narrowest of edges – less than 0.25cm (¹⁄₁₆in) if you can manage.

9 Take the front body shape of your fox and turn it pattern side up. Pin the completed face into position on the fox head then using your sewing machine sew all around the shape, about 0.5cm (⅛in) from the edge.

10 Position the front body shape and the back body shape together, patterned sides together and pin to secure. Using your machine, sew them together, leaving the bottom edge open.

Chunk!

11 Trim any excess fabric that lies beyond your stitching line, paying particular care to the areas of the ears and tail – but be careful not to trim so close that you chop through your sewing. Then turn your fox right side out.

12 Stuff the cushion with wadding (batting). Starting at the tip of the tail, pop small balls of stuffing into the cushion. Keep your long, blunt object handy to help guide the stuffing into the far corners and narrow bits of the fox shape.

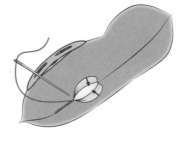

I inadvertently overstuffed my cushion, resulting in a super-firm fox. Remember that this fella is supposed to be a comfort item! Don't go overboard with wadding (batting) but do ensure that every part of the fox is sufficiently plump.

Time for Turning

This step is simple, but it is time consuming. Your fox shape has lots of pointy bits that require some extra attention when turning right side out. To save time and a whole heap of fiddling, enlist the help of your trusty up-ended knitting needle or chopstick, using it to tease out the corners of your fox shape gently.

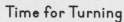

13 Create an inward fold on the bottom open edge and pin it in place. Using either a needle and thread or your sewing machine, sew up the last remaining seam. Finally, name your new fox friend and introduce him to your sofa!

MEET THE MAKER: Michelle Aaron

Michelle Aaron is the archetypal busy girl. She looks after her family, runs a successful business and is a keen crafter. When she's not baking delectable cakes or spending time with her daughter, Hannah, Michelle can be found in front of her sewing machine, growing her collection of soft plush and interior accessory designs. Michelle's textile creations always have bags of character and humour.

Tool of choice: My sewing machine – I'm not patient enough to sew by hand

Inspired by: Kids and the fantastically weird characters they come up with – one of my daughter's best is Loaf, a cat that's also a loaf of bread

Crafting soundtrack: 50s rock 'n' roll – or Nick Cave's *Let Love In*

Favourite designer: I love illustrator and designer Julie West

Favourite crafty snack: I don't usually snack when crafting – I snack all day, but just not while crafting!

Interesting fact: I own a 1950s cake shop called Auntie M's Cake Lounge (the cakes aren't from the 50s though, they're fresh!)

Most treasured possession: My daughter's amazing artwork

STITCH IT UP A NOTCH

- This project has given you the confidence to 'wing it' – to play around with designs and just see what happens. Harness that approach and you will get far. Now you can take these steps and apply them to all sorts of projects. Develop this new adventurous side and test out your ideas. Make other shapes, create more couch-friendly animal buddies! Maybe you could make a giant owl pillow? I've always fancied one of those …

- As well as cushions, the same techniques can be used on a smaller scale to make children's toys. A quirky and characterful handmade fox or owl would make a far lovelier gift than a boring shop-bought bear. When making toys, it's a good idea to double up your stitching so it withstands plenty of rough and tumble, and of course, always use washable fabrics and stuffing!

PUT YOUR FEET UP POUFFE

by Madness of Many

I don't know about you, but in my house, cushions and soft furnishings far outweigh crockery – and even cutlery! In those rare moments when I steal away some quiet time at home, I do love to be comfy. Intended for use as a pouffe or as a giant cushion, this handmade interior accessory will surely become one of your favourite rainy-day comfort items. Cosy down and snuggle up, baby!

Project Notes

I would love to say that I was pleased as punch with my performance during my pouffe lesson – but I have to put my hands up and admit that this just may have been a tiny bit of a crafting calamity! Had Kim not come to my rescue at several points of the project, I would have run into trouble. As it is though, I love my pouffe (even with its lumps, bumps, loose stitches and puckers!). They add character, right?

Madness of Many is the creative venture of Kimberly Diamond. I visited her seaside home-studio for my pouffe sewing lesson, and she held my hand all the way! Turn to the end of the project to discover a little more about her.

Pleased as punch... ☐
Crafting calamity... ☑

Get ready to show off...

❀ your basic pattern cutting skills ❀ your pinning skills ❀ your machine sewing skills ❀ those nimble fingers ❀ your patience

SEWING BOX ESSENTIALS

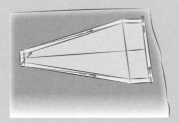

- ❀ Card or paper
- ❀ Compass
- ❀ Fabric, 1m x 60cm (1yd x 24in)
- ❀ Wadding (batting)
- ❀ 2 buttons, 4–5cm (1½–2in) in diameter
- ❀ Mattress needle
- ❀ Basic tool kit (see Getting Started)

1 Trace the supplied template (see Templates) onto the paper or card, giving you a blunt triangle-shaped pattern piece, which includes the seam allowance.

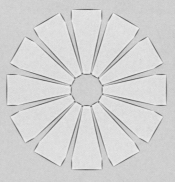

2 Using your pattern, cut 24 blunt triangle-shaped segments from your fabric.

3 Arrange 12 segments pattern side down into a ring. This shape will become the top of your pouffe. Then arrange the other 12 segments pattern side down into a second ring to become the bottom of your pouffe. Both rings will have a circular gap at the centre.

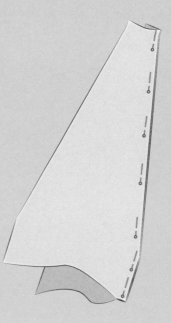

4 Pin your fabric segments together. Start by taking two segments, place them pattern side to pattern side and pin neatly on the right-hand side of the shape (pinheads facing upwards towards the narrowest end of the segment). Continue round ring 1, pinning on the right-hand side of the shape all the time. When all segments are pinned, get going on ring 2.

Ever–Decreasing Circles
It's best to measure the two circles in turn in case any slight variations in the two pouffe halves have occurred.

Chunk!

5 Using your sewing machine, sew the pieces of ring 1 together with a 1cm (⅜in) seam allowance and with your fabric hanging to the left. Then do the same with ring 2. Your stitched segments will now resemble two skirts – or volcanoes!

8 Place ring 1 on your lap with the mouth of the volcano on your knee. Your knee will be poking through the hole.

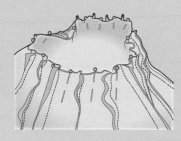

9 Pin the small circle of fabric into the hole of ring 1. Be careful not to pin the fabric to your clothing. To avoid getting tangled up, make sure all excess threads are hanging downwards and are not accidentally pinned into the circle. Repeat steps 8 and 9 for ring 2.

Top to Bottom
Make absolutely sure that you sew from the very top of the segment to the very bottom. If you accidentally leave any gaps at the top of your segments they will cause problems later.

10 Using your sewing machine, sew both the small circles into the mouths of the respective volcanoes.

6 Taking ring 1 first, measure the distance from one side of the volcano 'mouth' to the other to gauge a rough circumference of the circular hole at the centre. Then do the same with ring 2.

7 Add 2cm (¾in) to the rough circumference measurements you just took, and use a compass to make two paper templates. Use the templates to cut out two circles from your fabric.

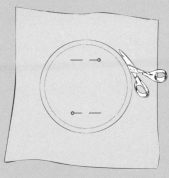

Chunk!

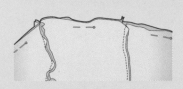

11 Now you have two full circles all ready, it's time to sew the two halves of your pouffe together. Position them on top of one another pattern side to pattern side, making sure your edges are lined up neatly, and pin to secure.

15 Using a mattress needle threaded with very strong thread, strong yarn or double thickness embroidery thread, position one of the large buttons in the centre of the pouffe and sew it on, pulling the thread through to the underside of the pouffe. Repeat as necessary, pulling the thread tight to create a button stud effect and tie off securely.

12 With the two halves safely secured together, sew all around the outside, about 1cm (⅜in) in from the edge – but leave a gap of approximately 20cm (8in) to allow you to turn it through and stuff it.

13 With the sewing complete, turn the fabric right side out through the gap in your stitching, then stuff with wadding (batting).

Smooth Stuffing
Due to the size of the pouffe and the time it will take to fill the cover, you will be tempted to tear big balls of stuffing but try not to rush this process or you will end up with a lumpy pouffe. Tease out the fibres to make even, fluffy dollops.

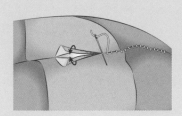

14 Once your pouffe is full of stuffing, you need to sew up the gap on the edge of your circle seam. It's too awkward to do this on the machine, so make an inward fold, pin in place then hand stitch.

 *Be prepared for some hard work here. You might even need some assistance. Two pairs of hands and a couple of strong arms sure do come in handy. Depending on your fabric and on how firmly you have stuffed your pouffe, it will take some force to work the mattress needle through.*

Chunk!

16 Sew the other large button on the underside of your pouffe, covering your thread knot. And now it's time to put your feet up!

MEET THE MAKER:
Kimberly Diamond

Artist and maker Kimberly Diamond (aka Madness of Many) designs and creates tongue-in-cheek textile pieces with a mischievous sense of humour. Locally, she is best known for her handcrafted 'guilt-free taxidermy' pieces. Mounted on wooden plaques, Kim's plush animal heads cause quite a stir at Made in the Shade HQ. Kim's work embodies a reuse and upcycle ethic and she often draws inspiration from woodland creatures – and quirky robot men.

Tool of choice: Scissors – I have a pair of fabric scissors tattooed on my arm!

Inspired by: Vintage fabric designs, charity shop treasure, buttons, thrifting and a desire to replace mass-produced items with handmade versions

Most treasured possession: Jeffrey, my fox taxidermy

Crafting companion: I'm an *X-Files* addict!

Favourite artists and designers: Dave McKean, Yoshitaka Amano and Jen Wang

Favourite crafting snack: Crunchy-nut cereal

Interesting fact: I once painted a naked person on stage at a gig in London

STITCH IT UP A NOTCH

- The easiest way to customize your pouffe is to experiment with fabric remnants. Make a patchwork-style pouffe using 24 different fabric segments or try making a self-coloured pouffe where the button studs become the focal point.

- By varying the amount and firmness of the wadding, you can create interiors items with slightly different functions. Stuff your pouffe very well with a substantial wadding to make the perfect footstool – or stuff your pouffe with a soft wadding to make a giant pillow instead!

Guerilla Crafting: Sewing's Secret Underground

The busy girl's brain is constantly a-bustle with to-dos, must-dos and will-do-one-days. Permanently pre-occupied and forever crammed full, her brain is hard pushed to keep up. At home, at work, on the street – she is bombarded with information. A lack of free time to relax and unwind makes for a pent-up person and, to keep from throwing a stress-induced 'wobbler', it's important to schedule in some fun. When you spend the best part of your day running round chasing your own tail, it's all too easy to forget what fun is. No matter how pressing our schedules are, we must, must, must allow ourselves time to be a little bit naughty, to let of steam and have a giggle. Heck! Other people do it. And … some people do it in a wonderfully positive, exciting and very public way.

Guerilla Art Defined

Don't be scared of the term 'guerilla craft'. Author and guerilla artist Keri Smith helpfully classifies guerilla art as, 'any anonymous work (including, but not limited to graffiti, signage, performance, additions and decoration)'. Guerilla craft is inclusive, it's free and it's accessible and it's there for the embracing.

Anonymous Interventions

Imagine my delight to happen upon a love heart marked on the pavement in gum on my way to meet a friend. Or the smile that crept across my face when I spotted a wall's worth of illustrated flies pasted next to a 'No Fly Posters' sign on the side of a shop. Or the gleeful little exclamation I made aloud when I found a tiny painting sitting inside the ticket machine of my local cinema. These instances of guerilla art are little messages, reminders that no matter how immersed in my busy schedule I am, I do still have that capacity to be surprised and amazed. Enjoy and appreciate the unexpected, why don't you? These public acts of creativity serve as happy little jolts – memos that good things happen and that there are creative people around, finding time to add a bit of humour and beauty to the community. We will never know who these sneaky joy-spreading Petes are – but if we just take a look around, we will feel the benefits of their efforts.

I first discovered guerilla crafting thanks to a link I made on a social networking site. In 2004, I made online 'friends' with a renegade street craft troupe from the US called Knitta Please. The Knittas were installing their knitted graffiti pieces on anything and everything that stood still in their hometown – from railings and bollards to cars and buildings. Excited, moved and inspired by their pioneering 'knitting graffiti' concept, I got in touch and told them just how wonderful I thought they were. The more I interacted with them, the more excited I became. There was nothing left to do but get involved. For one whole year, I spent my time sneaking round my local area under the cover of darkness and the guise of The Green Garter (ssssh, don't tell!). My efforts to decorate my urban environment were positively paltry in comparison with trailblazers like Knitta Please, but nevertheless, I got a real thrill from popping cosies onto parked bicycle seats, woolly sleeves onto door handles and mini graffiti tags onto trees and railings.

Take a break from yourself for a while. Step away from the jam-packed calendar and shake off the busy girl label for a moment. If you're already using craft to add variety and balance to your life or as a means to change your career path, then who's to say you can't use craft to change your community or to pop a magical moment into

someone else's day? Get involved with fun guerilla craft activities. Ill-fitting camouflage get-up is not compulsory and neither must you end up on the wrong side of the law! There are plenty pretty acts of crafty kindness you can share anonymously with unwitting strangers. Why should the knitters have all the fun? We budding Sewing Susan's can just as easily get in on the guerilla crafting act! Take your sewing onto the street and share your ideas, get stuff off your chest, enrich your day – and someone else's.

Reap What You Sew

Who would have thought that sewing could be such a thrill? Six project ideas to get your guerilla crafting campaign underway ...

1. Pick a neighbour or select an address randomly from the phone book. Package up your favourite craft pattern with a note inviting the recipient to discover their inner crafter. You just might be inspiring someone with creative aspirations to take the first step to making.

2. Gather together some glass jars from your recycling bucket. Clean them up and pop a selection of unwanted craft supplies inside – buttons, ribbons, trimmings. Pop a handwritten luggage label round the neck of the jar reading 'A crafty gift for you' – or similar message. Leave the jar in a public place and go about your business knowing that someone will be thrilled to find your present when/where they least expect it.

3. Got some fabric going spare? Next time you're de-cluttering your fabric stash, keep a few lengths aside and stitch up some basic cushions. Leave them on the seats on public transport or on a park bench. Warm the bottom of a stranger!

4. Embroider uplifting messages, lines of poetry or song lyrics onto old sheets and tablecloths and hang them in public places for all to see.

5. Public toilets can be depressing and generally unpleasant places to be. Pick up some secondhand towels from your local charity shop, stitch in a pretty motif or clever slogan and leave them folded neatly on the sink-top.

6. Create a temporary craft stall on top of a bollard or on a window ledge. Label everything, 'FREE'. Leave your display to be discovered by passers by.

PLEATS-APLENTY DUVET SKIRT

by Miss Lottie Lou

Clothes shopping can be fun, but when a busy girl is juggling work, social life and the demands of a hectic household, sometimes spending an afternoon trawling the shops is the last thing she needs. Bypass the bargain hunters and spend a much more productive afternoon in the serenity of your craft room making your very own retro-style box pleat skirt. In the spirit of make do and mend, this stylish gem is made from a repurposed duvet cover, so, it's practically free too!

Project Notes

When Charlotte showed me the garment I'd be making, I had my doubts but despite my initial fears, I thoroughly enjoyed my first foray into dressmaking. My inability to measure, mark or cut in a straight line was problematic at points, but contrary to what they say about every millimetre counting in dressmaking, my skirt turned out just fine (well, the front is slightly longer than the back and the waist is a little big, but apart from that, it's perfect!).

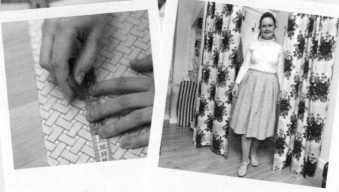

Clothing designer Charlotte Newell aka Miss Lottie Lou welcomed me to her retro-styled showroom for this thrifty skirt-making session. Find out more about Charlotte's business and her passion for 50s style at the end of the project.

Pleased as punch... ☑

Crafting calamity... ☐

Get ready to show off...
❀ your measuring and marking skills ❀ your machine sewing skills
❀ you basic hand sewing skills ❀ a little bit of mathematical know-how!

Preparing Your Fabric

Bag yourself a single duvet cover from your local thrift store, or pinch one from your granny's airing cupboard. Pick one with a great retro pattern. Wash and iron it so it's crisp and fresh for use. Cut off the strip of poppers/buttons from the bottom edge. Cut up both side seams to separate the two halves of the cover. Trim all edges to remove the seam allowances, stitches and overlocking.

Taking Measurements

• With a measuring tape, take your waist measurement. Whatever the measurement, add 2cm (¾in). This will be the waist measurement you'll go on to use in the project.
• Decide how wide you want your finished waistband to be. Multiply that measurement by two, then add 1cm (⅜in). You can make a substantial band, or a narrower one, depending on your build.

I plumped for a fairly narrow band, as I'm quite short. I felt a thicker waistband might swamp me a little bit. I decided, when making my skirt, on a 2.5cm (1in) waistband. I multiplied that figure by two to give 5cm (2in) and then I added 1cm (⅜in) to arrive at a final waistband width measurement of 6cm (2⅜in).

• To calculate the length of your skirt, measure from your waist down to where you want your skirt to stop. Add 2cm (¾in) for hem allowance. Then, subtract the width of your waistband to give the real length measurement of the skirt. E.g. (taking the metric example) Waistband (5cm + 1cm) = 6cm. Desired length (72cm + 2cm) = 74cm. Actual length (74cm − 6cm) = 68cm.

1 To cut your waistband section, measure and mark a rectangle shape on the reverse of the fabric with tailor's chalk or dressmaker's pen – taking your final waist measurement and final waistband width measurement (see box, opposite) as dimensions of the rectangle. Cut out the rectangle with pinking shears.

Super Snips
When working with cotton fabrics, pinking shears offer a quick and inexpensive alternative to fancy overlocker machines. If you're not sure what your fabric is made of or you're not sure whether it's suitable for use with pinking shears, cut a test strip. If the fabric doesn't fray, you're good to go with your chosen material – and with no need to overlock!

2 To cut the skirt section, lay the fabric flat, pattern side down. Measure and mark another rectangle – this time, the final waist measurement times two and final length measurement (see box, opposite) are the dimensions. Cut out the shape with pinking shears.

The dimensions of my rectangle are 172 x 74cm (68 x 29in). This is because my final waist measurement was 86cm (34in), which is doubled, and the final length measurement was 74cm (29in).

Chunk!

3 To create the first of your box pleats on the skirt, mark 1cm (⅜in) in from each edge of the skirt fabric (at the waistband end) then fold the fabric in half, pattern side to pattern side. With a pin, mark the centre point of the fabric where the fold is.

For now, you're using the pin as a marker only. Make sure you can still move both sides of the skirt and that you haven't pinned them together by accident!

4 Unfold the fabric and lay it out pattern side down. Taking the marker pin as your starting point, measure and mark 8cm (3in) on either side of the pin with chalk/dressmaker's pen.

5 To create the pleat, fold in the fabric from the left-hand mark to meet the marker in the middle and pin to secure. Then, do the same again, folding in the fabric from the right-hand mark.

Productive Pleating
If you are super-short on time or short on fabric – the bigger the box pleat, the quicker the project becomes and the less fabric you use up. You could measure 10cm (4in) from the mark, or even 12cm (5in) to make bigger pleats.

6 Take your waistband section and fold it in half widthways, wrong sides together.

7 Then, fold in half lengthways. Place a marker pin in the lengthways fold in order to mark the mid-point of the waistband and the secure the widthways fold.

8 Match up the mid-point on the waistband with the centre of the box pleat you just created. Pin the waistband to the skirt section pattern side to pattern side to secure.

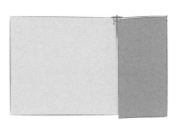

9 Hold up your skirt fabric or lay it out flat. Take the right-hand end of the skirt fabric and fold it in to meet the mid-point you've marked on the waistband and first box pleat. Mark the new fold in the fabric with a pin. This point will become the centre of your next box pleat.

10 Repeat steps 4 and 5 to make the second box pleat.

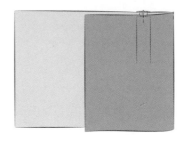

11 To make the third box pleat, take the centre point of box pleat 1 to meet the centre point of box pleat 2. Mark the new fold with a pin as before. This will be the centre point of box pleat 3.

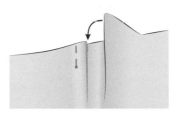

12 Create your box pleat exactly as before (see steps 4 and 5).

13 So far you have made one pleat in the centre of the skirt and two on the right-hand side of this. Repeat steps 9 to 12 to create two more box pleats on the left-hand side of the skirt, so you have five box pleats altogether.

Chunk!

Making Adjustments

At this stage, lie the whole skirt flat, pattern side up. Check that the skirt width hasn't become smaller than the waistband length due to the box pleating. If it has, either remove some pleats, or alter the width of the box pleats. If the skirt section is bigger than the waistband, then there is no need to fiddle with pleats but you will have to get rid of the excess fabric. Measure the excess and mark a guide line of the same width down the entire length of the skirt. Cut along the guide line using pinking shears.

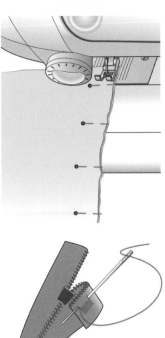

14 Turn the skirt pattern side down again and pin the waistband all the way along, making sure the top edge of the waistband is lying neat with the top edge of the skirt fabric. With your sewing machine, stitch the waistband to the skirt, 0.5cm (⅛in) from the edge, using the edge of the presser foot as a guide. Once the waistband has been stitched on, flip it up and iron it in position.

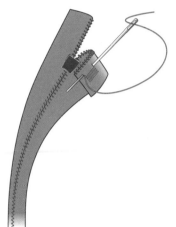

15 Take your zip and fold the excess flaps beneath the zip stopper to the reverse side of the zip and sew a few hand stitches in to secure in place. Once you've done that, open the zip.

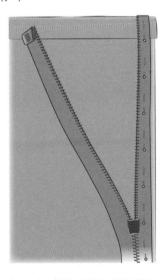

16 With the skirt fabric pattern side up, take the left side of your zip, flip it over wrong side up and lay it along the edge of the fabric – right side of fabric facing the right side of zip. Make sure the top of the zip is edge to edge with the top of the waistband. Pin to secure.

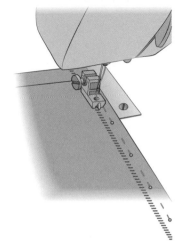

17 Change the presser foot on your sewing machine to an invisible zipper foot. Stitch the first side of your zip to the skirt fabric, stopping where the zip teeth end.

The invisible zipper foot makes life just that little bit easier when stitching in concealed zips. The attachment allows you to stitch the zip in very close to the edge of the zip with precision. Some sewing machines will come with this foot but if yours doesn't – fret not. You can buy an invisible zipper foot inexpensively from your local haberdasher. A worthy purchase!

18 With one side of the concealed zip now sewn into the skirt, fold the skirt in half, pattern side to pattern side, then position the remaining loose end of the zip along the other edge of the skirt, lining up edge to edge as before. Pin to secure.

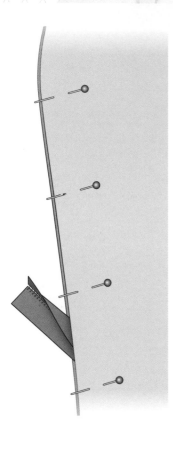

19 Do up the zip. Keeping the loose end of the zip out of your way, pin the seam of the skirt together.

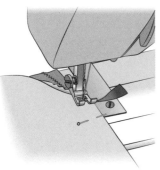

20 Pop the standard presser foot back on your machine. Using a 0.5cm (⅛in) seam again and using the edge of the foot as a guide, stitch the edges of the skirt together. With your iron, press the seam open from below the zip right to the bottom edge of the skirt.

Chunk!

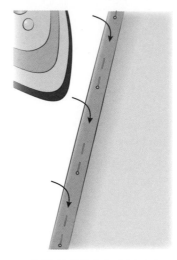

21 To add the skirt hem, fold the bottom edge of the skirt up 1cm (⅜in). Repeat, folding up another 1cm (⅜in). Pin to secure, working all round the hem edge. Iron in place then remove the pins.

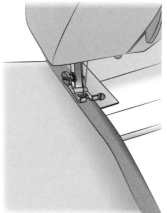

22 Sew the hem, 0.5cm (⅛in) from the edge, all the way round the bottom edge of the skirt.

23 Take any excess thread showing on the pattern side of the skirt and thread it through to the reverse side. Tie off and chop it off. Check the rest of the garment for excess threads, tie them off and trim.

MEET THE MAKER: Charlotte Newell

Charlotte Newell, aka Miss Lottie Lou, fully embraces vintage lifestyle and at just 22, she is channelling her passions and making her mark on the vintage clothing circuit. The owner of her own bricks-and-mortar shop and studio, Charlotte designs and makes vintage-style garments for customers to buy off the peg and also runs a successful bespoke business. Feminine, fun, pretty and practical, Charlotte's collections include fabulous high-waisted sailor pants, 1940s-style wrap dresses and gorgeous two-piece summer suits.

Tool of choice: My overlocker – it makes a fabulous purring sound!

Inspired by: My mother, the 1950s, vintage patterns, vintage magazines, make do and mend

Crafting soundtrack: My DJ dad's mix CDs of music from the 40s and 50s

Favourite designer: Vivienne Westwood

Favourite crafty snack: Cakes and sweeties! I also drink a lot of green tea

Most treasured possession: My car – a flame red 1989 Mini called Gav

STITCH IT UP A NOTCH

- If you are feeling adventurous, and you think you have the stamina, you could always experiment with different sized box pleats. Creating small ones all round the waistband of the skirt gives a beautifully full and swooshy result. Bigger ones make for a more structural, tailored look.

- Try making a small version for a child, making the length a bit shorter. If you have a daughter you could even make co-ordinating skirts for you to wear to out together! And perhaps her favourite rag doll could have her own mini version too made from the offcuts … Cute!

THE BUSY GIRL'S BAG

by Angharad Jefferson

I rarely leave the house with just one bag – I usually have a tote on one shoulder, a satchel on the other and a handbag hooked on whichever finger happens to be free. Every busy girl needs a Busy Girl's Bag. Not only does the clever fold-over design keep your belongings safe, but concealed within are three good-sized pockets fit for all your must-haves. Easily customizable, this bag is functional *and* beautiful.

Project Notes

I absolutely adore this design. Seeing my Busy Girl's Bag take shape as the project progressed was really, really exciting. In between giggles, Angharad had to step in and take control of my sewing as I struggled to get the hang of chain stitch. I don't know how many times I had to unpick my embroidery! Sewing the bag together proved quite tricky in places but I'm looking forward to practising this project over and over until I master it. In the end – with Angharad's expertise at hand – I am pleased as punch with my bag!

Angharad travelled to the Made in the Shade HQ specially to hold a one-to-one bag-making lesson with me. A truly fabulous textile designer and needlework whizz, Angharad wowed me with her stitching prowess! Meet her at the end of the project.

Pleased as punch... ☑
Crafting calamity... ☐

Get ready to show off...
❀ your measuring and cutting skills ❀ your hand embroidery skills
❀ your basic machine sewing skills ❀ those nimble fingers ❀ your eye for detail ❀ your imagination

SEWING BOX ESSENTIALS

- ✿ Heavyweight fabric, at least 30 x 61cm (12 x 24in) (for the exterior)
- ✿ Mid-weight fabric, 1m (1yd) (for the interior and embroidered panel)
- ✿ Heavyweight fusible interfacing, 1.5m (1½yd)
- ✿ Zip, 80cm (30in)
- ✿ A piece of non-bleed tissue paper or newsprint
- ✿ Fine permanent marker pen
- ✿ Embroidery hoop
- ✿ Embroidery needle and threads
- ✿ Long, thin, blunt object (up-ended knitting needle or chopstick)
- ✿ Basic tool kit (see Getting Started)

Choosing Your Fabrics

For this project, you need two different fabrics – one for the outer body of your bag and one for the interior and pockets. Angharad advised using a thick, stable wool fabric for the body of the bag and she suggested using linen for the interior. If you can't get your hands on a good wool fabric, think about using thick upholstery remnants or a quality curtain fabric. You could always use a non-stretch cotton fabric for the interior – think about repurposing vintage bed linen or an old linen tablecloth if you can find one big enough.

1 First, prepare all the fabric pieces you will need to make your bag. Measure and mark the measurements given in the Cutting List (see opposite) onto your fabrics with dressmaker's pen and cut your pieces using good, sharp fabric shears.

2 Iron the interfacing pieces (following the manufacturer's instructions) onto the back of their same-sized fabric pieces.

The heavyweight interfacing will add a rigidity and stability to the fabrics and give a great final finish to your bag.

Role Call
To keep track of which fabric piece is which, mark letters on the back as given in the Cutting List (see opposite). Either use dressmaker's pen or pin little paper pieces onto the backs of the fabric pieces. You will be glad of this later when we come to construct the design.

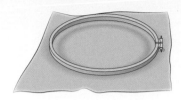

4 Take fabric piece B and place it centrally on top of the inner hoop of the embroidery hoop. Carefully place the outer hoop, over the top. Tighten up the screw on the hoop ensuring the fabric is taught.

5 Pin the traced design onto the taught, hooped fabric and use your embroidery needle and threads to embroider the image as desired (see below) – sewing through the paper and the fabric. Once you're satisfied with your embroidery, tear away the paper.

Chunk!

Chunk!

3 Choose the image you want to embroider onto your bag – you can use Angharad's template (see Templates), trace an old photograph, or draw your own freehand design. Using a fine permanent marker, trace your image onto the non-bleed tissue paper or newsprint.

Using a permanent marker for your drawing will mean that the ink stays on the paper, rather than transferring onto the thread or fabric. Clever!

Embroidering Your Image

Embroidery isn't about following a prescribed set of stitch instructions determined by someone else in order to produce an identikit design – it is simply about drawing with your needle. It's up to you how intricate you want your embroidery to be. Which stitches you use, which marks you make to interpret a design, is entirely up you. To keep yourself from getting tangled up though, it's probably best to stick to a mixture of chain stitch, running stitch and back stitch to begin with. Experiment with the thickness of your threads to achieve your desired look and texture. If you need a guide to get you started, look at the photograph of my bag as a starting point. You will get into your own stitching groove with practice.

6 With the embroidered panel complete we can now construct the bag. For the front panel, take fabric pieces A and B, place them pattern side to pattern side and pin along one short side to secure. Ensure your embroidered motif is upside down in order that it will fold down into position in the next step.

8 For the inner panel, position the zip onto the right-hand long edge of fabric piece C, right sides together. Pin to secure then stitch straight down the right edge from the top of the zip to the bottom.

9 Position the other side of the zip onto fabric piece D. Align neatly with fabric piece C, again right sides together. Pin and then stitch down the other side of the zip.

7 Using your sewing machine set to a plain stitch, sew fabric pieces A and B together, 1cm (⅜in) from the edge, then iron the seams open. You now have one long strip of exterior fabric with your embroidery panel attached at the bottom, with the motif facing up in the right direction.

10 With your iron, press the zip placket (fabric piece D), folding the fabric to conceal the zip. Press again to hold in place.

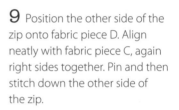

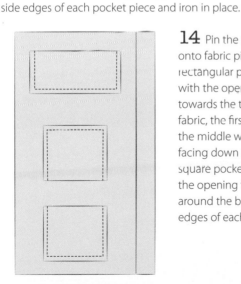

11 Stitch the first and last 6cm (2½in) of the zip placket down in a rectangle formation for strength.

Chunk!

12 Turn in a double fold (approx 1cm/⅜in) into the top edge of each of the pockets, fabric pieces F (x2) and G. Iron in place then machine stitch to secure.

13 Next, turn in folds (again, approx 1cm/⅜in) into the bottom and side edges of each pocket piece and iron in place.

14 Pin the pockets in position onto fabric piece C. Pin the rectangular pocket at the top with the opening facing up towards the top edge of the fabric, the first square pocket in the middle with the opening facing down and then the final square pocket at the bottom with the opening facing up. Stitch around the bottom and side edges of each pocket.

Chunk!

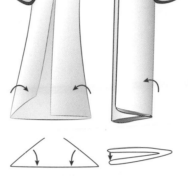

15 Your bag needs handles. Take fabric pieces E and fold each handle in half widthways and then iron. Using the fold as a centre guide line, fold in the edges at either side into the centre guide line and iron again. Now, fold widthways again, iron then pin in place. You will now have two long thin tube-like strips measuring approximately 115 x 2.5cm (45¼ x 1in).

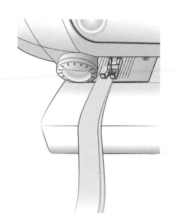

16 Stitch down the open edge of each strap from the top to the bottom to secure your folds.

17 Lay the bag outer right side down then fold it inwards roughly into thirds with the embroidered panel on top. Position the first fabric handle close to the bottom edge of the bag, making sure the ends sit neatly beneath the embroidered panel. Mark the position of the handles then open the bag up and pin the handles in place.

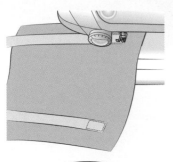

18 Stitch the handle down, turn then stitch again to secure until you have made a rectangle shape, as you did when securing the zip ends in step 11.

19 Fold the bag outer up again, as before, and position the second handle on the back of the bag (in line with the handle on the front). Mark the position then open the bag up, pin the handle in place then stitch. Stitch again 15cm (6in) up to secure.

Adding these extra stitches to the back handle not only ensures your handle is absolutely secure, but it also creates a handy loop – ideal for carrying your umbrella. Nifty!

Chunk!

20 Now you have assembled all your bag segments, it's time to stitch the bag together. With the handles facing in and with the zip open, pin the outer and inner panels of the bag together, right sides facing. Sew all around the edge of the bag approximately 1cm (⅜in) from the edge.

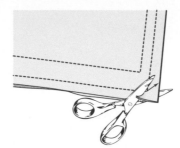

21 Trim the corners in a neat diagonal then turn the bag right side out, through the open zip. Using a long thin, blunt ended object, push the corners out to neat points.

22 Iron the entire bag. Spending some time ironing your bag will keep your folds in place and will give a beautifully neat finish.

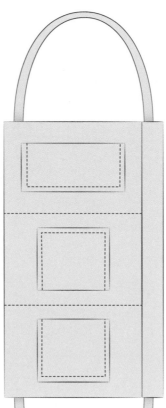

23 Go back to the sewing machine and stitch along the folds of the bag (up to the zip) to give them added definition. Fill up your Busy Girl Bag with all your busy girl 'can't-do-withouts' and use!

MEET THE MAKER:
Angharad Jefferson

Angharad Jefferson is a textile artist and super-talented designer-maker. Using her specially customized sewing machine, Angharad designs and creates intricate freestyle machine embroidery pieces. Her work is most easily described as stitched illustration. She draws with a pencil then she draws with a needle. By combining marvellous detail with rich texture and vintage fabric backdrops, Angharad's work is instantly recognizable. Her work adorns the walls of rock stars!

Tool of choice: Needle and thread (I am old school)

Inspired by: The potential stored up in an HB pencil

Favourite designers/makers/artists: Fiona Douglas of bluebellgray, Chloe and Mhairi from bebaroque, Laura Vickers of Dear Prudence, and Cosima Sempill of Kitty and Dude

Most treasured possession: My little family

Crafting soundtrack: Mr B the Gentleman Rhymer

Favourite crafty tipple: Lipton tea – and plenty of it!

Interesting fact: I am descended from pirates

STITCH IT UP A NOTCH

- This bag is suitable for use as a craft bag, a work case, baby changing bag or even as an overnight make-up and toiletries 'roll' – but better still if you make several in different fabrics and with different embroidered motifs you can have one for all of these purposes… you will soon wonder how you ever got by without your Busy Girl's Bags!

- Customize your bag by using different fabric colours and patterns for your handles and inside pockets and experiment with different pocket closures.

- If you're nervous about trying freestyle embroidery (or you tried and it was a total crafting calamity), use waste canvas as a grid for a simpler cross stitch design instead (see Apples & Pears Apron).

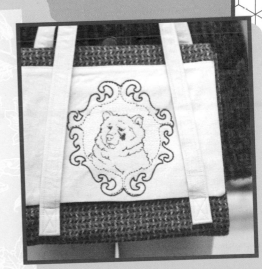

Making To Sell: Setting Up Shop at Craft Fairs

'Aah … Wouldn't it be great, one day, to run my own craft business,' you think to yourself in a rare moment of (relative) quiet as you gaze out of the bus window on your way to work. You know, with the right skills, a super-tight action plan, a load of hard work and an extra dollop of creative, go-getting oomph, over time, you might just be able to take those pipe dreams out of the confines of your imagination and plonk them into real life. Setting up a home studio like Susie Maroon or opening your own sewing shop front like Miss Lottie Lou needn't be out of reach.

As a busy girl, you will no doubt have a million other things to consider before you dive head first into starting your own full-blown craft enterprise. However, if you manage to slot regular sewing sessions into your otherwise crammed calendar, there is nothing to say that you can't dedicate some of your precious craft time to developing your skills, your ideas and perfecting your first original designs ready for sale. Harking back to the 'chunking' technique we talked about way back at the beginning of the book, you can apply this 'little-by-little' approach to your budding business aspirations too. Use the information in this feature to inform your future plans. Don't rush into taking your work to market. Lay the groundwork at your own pace and embark on your exciting new adventure as and when the time is right!

A great starting point for any aspiring craft retailer, your local craft fair circuit offers a window into running a business and gives you a taste of what works and what doesn't when trying to sell your designs. Before you do anything else though, research your market. Find out what and who is out there in craft land already. Who knows? When you have your first collection ready, the craft fair might just wind up being the springboard for your business you've been looking for.

Making For Fun Vs Making To Sell

Contrary to what you might think, making to sell differs considerably from making for fun. Your homespun creations now need to be transformed into marketable, saleable, handmade covetables. The quality of your materials and the finish of your work will be under close scrutiny from potential suppliers and customers, and the pressure under which you will be sewing when order deadlines loom might detract from the original enjoyment and feel of escape you enjoyed when sewing just for fun.

Now, that's not to say that running your own crafty business can't be fun too, but do understand that it's a whole new type of fun – maybe not as free and easy as you first expect! Tuning into the routine that works best for you takes some time. Suss out whether you are an early bird or a night owl. As your venture develops and grows you will implement systems and handy tricks to manage your time and make the most of peaks in productivity.

Spoilt for Choice

The lowly craft fair sure has come a long way over the last few years. We're through with singular notions of what a 'craft fair' is for starters. So many niche events are popping up in venues all over the land, some incorporating vintage fashion and lifestyle, food and drink, music and dancing and even pop-up teashops and cake lounges. We're spoilt for choice – as customers and as crafters. From ramshackle bring-and-buy sales lovingly thrust together on rickety tabletops in the leaky community hall to oh-so-slick design show booths constructed in loft galleries, the busy crafter has a task on her hands just deciding which forum might best suit her creative venture. Such is the variety of events that 'craft fair' is a barely suitable description of these crafty shopping affairs any more. Now we have a wealth of craft markets, boutique shopping events, DIY showcases, renegade marketplaces and veritable craft-o-ramas to enjoy!

Before you harness that excitement and go ahead and set up your stall right there in your town hall, stop awhile and have a little think about what you want to achieve first. What are you looking to get out of your craft fair experience? If you are developing your very first craft collection, it might be more important, initially, to encourage dialogue and generate interest around your work than to make lots and lots of sales. Customer comments and feedback from your peers are invaluable no matter how experienced a designer-maker you are – but it is particularly useful when starting out. You can bet your boots there will be a craft event in your neighbourhood that will suit your business and your personality.

The Perfect Fit

As a newbie to the craft community, navigating through screeds of craft fair listings to find the perfect forum for your fledgling business can be daunting and may well leave your head all in a whirl. Fret not. Cosy down in your comfy chair. Armed with a notepad and pen, a glass of your favourite fizz and maybe a nice biscuit for emergencies, set out to be methodical and thorough in your research. Once you've compiled a list of events, set to work finding out more about them. Search online for event websites, social networking profiles and

and getting to know how organizers tick. As a general rule, I'd advise exercising a little caution where there appears to be no application or vetting process in place at all. As a vendor you want to know that your work will sit well alongside that of the other sellers and you want to know that some care has been taken to showcase work of a certain standard and feel. If the organizer has no idea who is setting up shop at their event, how will they publicize the event effectively to reach the right customers and generate footfall?

Probably the most important element of your craft fair application is your product photography. Organizers do love to learn about the background and history of your creative venture, but ultimately they need to see what you sell. During the selection process, decisions about the quality, finish and overall aesthetic of submissions are usually made by looking at photographs on a computer screen. Not ideal, I know – it's difficult to fully understand a product until it has been touched and looked at in person – but you must aim to highlight the features of your products as best you can with the resources you have. Applicants who organize good-quality, attractive and well-lit shots of their products will always grab an organizer's attention. Do your work justice and represent it with as much care as you've taken to make it. There is no need to invest in professional photography services just yet! You can achieve satisfactory DIY results at home with a makeshift light box, background and a good digital camera. You never know, submit a top-notch product image with your application and you might even find your work used on the event's promotional materials.

archive press articles. Even the smallest craft event might be using free networks such as Twitter to promote their activities. Learn about the people behind the market. Are they designer-makers themselves? What experience do they have working with creative vendors and organizing events? Scope out the venue – is it well-located and handy for transport links? Have a little snoop around. The most effective way to learn about different craft fairs is, of course, to attend them. Pop along as a customer before booking a slot. Chat to the people in charge. Chat to the other vendors. Take mental note of what other handmade work is on offer and think about the price points in relation to your own. Does the fair cater for a particular type of customer or a particular type of maker? Is it traditional or more renegade in nature? Try to think objectively about your work. Your craft business won't necessarily go on to 'fit' at every event. In the early stages, you will need to conduct a whole heap of research. You'll need to define who your customers are. Find out how much money they typically spend at a craft fair. Try mentally to position your work in terms of style, quality, appeal and price. Where will your business sit in the wider craft community?

Taking the Plunge

So. You've decided it's time to try your luck selling your handmade wares at a craft fair, huh? Now, application processes will vary from fair to fair. Some will operate strict vetting procedures and hefty waiting lists while others will require no advance information from vendors at all and work on a first come, first served basis. When starting out, keep an open mind and experiment. Spend some time doing your research

DIY Realities

I've heard so many people tell stories about landing what they thought would be their dream job in the creative sphere, only to be faced with some harsh realities. Of course, it's wonderful to be immersed in work you love and being your own boss certainly has its up sides. However, especially when starting out, be prepared for some tough times. You'll likely be overworked yet stony broke and you'll find that your time is swallowed up quicker than ever. But! It's by no means all doom and gloom. There is nothing more satisfying than to receive positive recognition for your efforts – a note from a customer, an article in the press or glowing feedback from your peers.

Make a List, Check it Twice

So, you've been accepted to sell at your very first craft fair. You are excited, but you are in a pickle. Your craft area is in chaos and you are up to your neck in double-sided sticky tape. You've lost track of just what you were trying to do with the shredded tissue paper. And now the cat has stomped its claws through your freshly printed price list. Let's breathe for a moment.

Setting up shop for the first time at a craft fair can be a nerve-racking experience. Thinking back to the first time I trundled my little craft trolley into the event hall in my local library on the morning of my first fair, I remember all too vividly how scary it can be. My hands were clammy, my face was flushed and I was terrified that the other vendors would think I was an interloper, that the customers would hate my products and that I'd leave having sold nothing. As it turned out, the very opposite came to be true. I met loads of like-minded people some of whom remain very good friends. I received bucket loads of constructive feedback from everyone who visited my stand and by the end of the day, I'd sold out of my handmade soap bars.

Fore-armed is forewarned when it comes to craft fairs. Some care taken over planning ahead of the event is all that's required to make sure your day goes smoothly. With everything in hand, you can relax and enjoy yourself in amongst all the networking and selling!

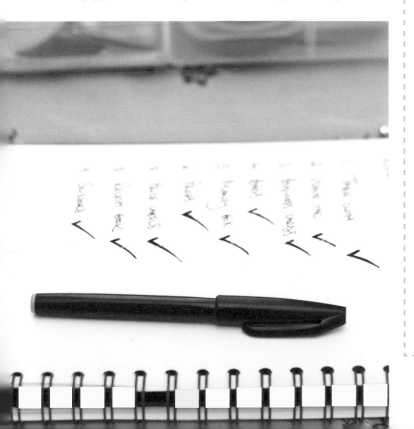

Keep Calm and Craft On

Some helpful hints for a smooth lead-up to the event ...

- Practise setting up your stall ahead of event day. Mark out the table size on the floor with tape. Play around with effective positioning and make sure everything fits. When you've decided on the perfect layout, make a little sketch of it and pop it into your craft fair kit, ready for event day.

- You don't need to invest in expensive banners to create exciting branding for your stall. With a little imagination you can produce great results with beautiful handwritten labels and price tags. If you're not confident with your handwriting, experiment with rubber stamps on vintage-style luggage tags. Ensure that your business name features visibly on your stall so that customers will be able to recognize you and your work when they spot you next time.

- Remember to tell your friends, family and colleagues that you are taking up a stall at the craft fair. They will want to show their support and even if they don't all buy from you, the hustle and bustle, chatter and laughter emanating from your stall will attract attention, potentially drawing more custom.

- Gauging how much stock to take along is a notoriously tricky aspect, but I suggest you try the following tactic. First, calculate the total amount of sales you need to make to cover your costs (travel, stall fee, parking etc.). Then, decide on a realistic target that, if met, you would leave feeling thoroughly pleased with. Always make sure you have enough stock to allow you to reach that target.

- Think about your customer-service approach. No one likes a pushy sales person, but making eye contact with your visitors and offering a warm smile or a polite, 'hello' will never cause objection. Always acknowledge your stall visitors. Engage them in conversation and offer snippets of information about your craft. Craft fair shoppers tend to be loyal shoppers – so get to know them and make a good impression!

Templates

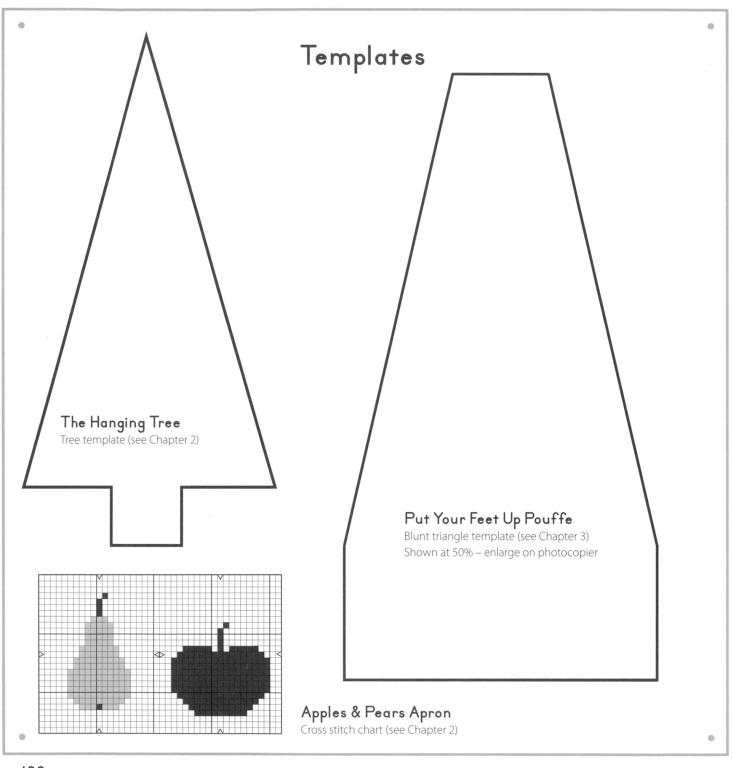

The Hanging Tree
Tree template (see Chapter 2)

Put Your Feet Up Pouffe
Blunt triangle template (see Chapter 3)
Shown at 50% – enlarge on photocopier

Apples & Pears Apron
Cross stitch chart (see Chapter 2)

The Busy Girl's Bag
Embroidery design template
(see Chapter 3)

Directory

Welcome to the Directory! Here you will find a categorized list of my favourite online resources, shops, blogs and crafty websites. Browse till your heart's content (or until you get boggly eyes and sore wrists!).

Inspirational Makers

Rachael Lamb
Hannah Zakari
www.hannahzakari.co.uk

Claire Brown
Miso Funky
www.misofunky.com

Kimberly Diamond
Madness of Many
www.madnessofmany.com

Kirsty Anderson
Wooden Tree
http://wooden-tree.blogspot.com

Jolene Crawford
http://preciouseast.
wordpress.com

Charlotte Newell
Miss Lottie Lou
http://misslottielou.blogspot.com

Susan Brown
Susie Maroon
www.susiemaroon.co.uk

Michelle Aaron
Covetables/Auntie M's Cake Lounge
www.covetables.co.uk

Angharad Jefferson
www.angharadjefferson.com

Great Suppliers

Donna Flower
www.donnaflower.com

Spinsters Emporium
www.spinstersemporium.co.uk

Liberty
www.liberty.co.uk

Gorgeous Shopping

Freddie's of Pinewood
www.freddiesofpinewood.co.uk

Love Me Again
http://lovemeagain.com

Revamp Vintage
www.revampvintage.com

Sewing Inspiration

Gertie's New Blog for Better Sewing
www.blogforbettersewing.com

Six and a Half Stitches
http://sixandahalfstitches.typepad.com

Sweet Sassafras
www.sweetsassafras.org

Indie Craft and Design

Meet Me At Mikes
http://meetmeatmikes.blogspot.com

Indie Quarter
www.indiequarter.com

Design*Sponge
www.designspongeonline.com

Craft Mafia
www.craftmafia.com

Craft City Melbourne
http://craftcitymelbourne.blogspot.com

Acknowledgments

Thank you to my husband, Garry, for looking after me so well and for agreeing to take on the role of book photographer. May this be the first team project of many. Thanks too, to Clare – my friend and business sidekick, for holding down the Made in the Shade fort while I was forever glued to my computer and for making such valued contributions to the book chapters and design. To the busy makers who took time out of their hectic schedules to welcome me into their homes and workspaces: you are inspirational. And, lucky for me, very patient! Thank you to my editor, Ame Verso, for remaining upbeat and positive throughout the process. Your support and guidance was invaluable. Finally, thank you to Jennifer Fox-Proverbs and the team at David & Charles for inviting me to write *The Busy Girl's Guide* and for being so open to my ideas. Particular thanks go to Ali Myer for embracing the 'novice writes a craft book' concept and to Mia Trenoweth for working so hard on the layout and design.

About the Author

Carrie Maclennan is co-owner of DIY creative business, Made in the Shade. A writer, shop owner and indie craft event organizer, she is the archetypal busy girl. She lives and works in Glasgow, Scotland and shares an apartment in the city's east end with her husband and enormous grey cat. With a background in music and media, Carrie has been working her local creative community for more than 10 years. She has been contributing to the growth of the indie craft 'scene' in Glasgow since 2004. She has a penchant for pretty frocks, an obsession with stationery and a long-time love of country music. Back in the days when she had some free time, she enjoyed guerilla crafting, making vintage-inspired bath and beauty products and running a craft and old-time music club – just for fun. This is her first book.

About Made in the Shade

Made in the Shade is a multi-faceted creative business based in Glasgow, Scotland. Run by indiepreneurs and vintage lifestyle lovers Carrie Maclennan and Clare Nicolson, Made in the Shade champions indie craft and design and provides a retail and promotional platform for emerging designer-makers. By hosting large-scale boutique shopping events, Made in the Shade helps new creative ventures establish a retail presence and encourages customers to shop handmade over high street. The Made in the Shade event is no ordinary craft fair. By coupling the best indie craft vendors with retro gala-style features, live music, public crafting and drop-in workshops, the Made in the Shade gals successfully shook up the notion of 'craft' in their hometown.

Carrie and Clare now run a bricks-and-mortar shop in Glasgow's west end called The Maisonette. An extension of the original Made in the Shade event, the shop offers customers handmade homewares, wearables, gifts, stationery and crafty lifestyle products while also offering fledgling businesses and would-be suppliers support and guidance through the process of working with retailers. The pair also manage a varied programme of workshops at their HQ where complete beginners and curious crafters can learn about dressmaking and bookbinding, crochet and printing – and everything in between.

The Made in the Shade Maisonette
Upper Floor De Courcy's Arcade
21 Cresswell Lane
Glasgow, G12 8AA
www.wearemadeintheshade.com
mail@wearemadeintheshade.com
Find us on Facebook – search for 'The Maisonette'
Follow us on Twitter at @madeintheshade1

Index